Visual Needs

**Olga Miller and Adam Ockelford, with
Nita Odedra and Jonathon Bolt**

LONDON • NEW YORK

Continuum International Publishing Group
The Tower Building
11 York Road
London
SE1 7NX

15 East 26th Street
New York
NY 10010

www.continuumbooks.com

British Library Cataloguing-in-Publication Data
A catalogue record for this book is available from the British Library.

ISBN: 0 8264 7838 7 (paperback)

Typeset by Servis Filmsetting Ltd, Manchester
Printed and bound in Great Britain by MPG Books Ltd, Bodmin,
Cornwall

Contents

Visual Needs

Acknowledgements

Nita Odedra

Nita Odedra is an experienced Optometrist with an interest in children and eye-health policy. In addition to her work for the Royal National Institute of the Blind, Nita has worked as a member of multidisciplinary teams in the UK and overseas.

Jonathon Bolt

Jonathon Bolt is a teacher with a specialist qualification in visual impairment. Jonathon is a member of a large Peripatetic Service catering for the needs of children and young people who have a severe visual loss or impairment. Jonathon works closely with children and their families as woll as advising professionals.

Introduction

At least four in every 10,000 children born in UK will be diagnosed as severely visually impaired or blind by their first birthday. The most common cause of sight problems in children is cortical visual impairment followed by hereditary and congenital optic nerve and retinal disorders.

This book, which we hope teachers, carers and parents will find equally helpful, deals with the development of vision and the possible needs of children who are visually impaired. However, because the first few years of life are so important in a child's development, we have often placed particular emphasis on the needs of children in the early years. We also wanted to acknowledge that this is an especially significant period for parents, particularly if they discover that their child has a serious visual impairment or indeed may have no sight at all. Total blindness is extremely rare so parents of babies who are blind often feel particularly isolated. Friends and relatives want to support as much as possible but sometimes parents need time to reflect and to grieve. It is also a time of hope, though, as one mother explained:

I had never met anyone who couldn't see, so when I was told my baby was blind I desperately wanted to know that

1

there were happy blind children who could do things like other children – and this has proved to be the case.

It is worth emphasizing that children who are visually impaired are as different from each other as any other children. The effects of visual loss (even if the eye condition is the same) can vary enormously from child to child.

But what counts as a visual impairment?

The World Health Organization (WHO) guidance for classifying levels of vision in childhood is based on three measures (Bowman, Bowman and Dulton 2001):

♦ Visual impairment – visual acuity less that 6/18 but better than or equal to 6/60 (see pp. 22–3)

♦ Severe visual impairment – visual acuity of less than 6/60 but better or equal to 3/60

♦ Blindness – visual acuity of less than 3/60

However, for some children these measures are not always particularly helpful, though they do have a status for purposes of registration within the UK. Registration is the process whereby certain financial benefits and entitlement to specialist services may be claimed by parents and carers on behalf of the child and later by individuals themselves. In early childhood functional vision may change rapidly so the WHO measures should be treated as a guide rather than an absolute. In terms of development and education it is more helpful to translate these measures into questions around a child's possible needs:

♦ Is the child likely to need additional help with dressing and eating skills?

♦ Is there a need to give specific consideration to lighting conditions either to reduce light/glare or to customize task lighting?

♦ Will the child need specialist mobility training to learn her way around?

♦ Should special consideration be given to stimulating vision?

♦ Is the child likely to need opportunities to learn through touch rather than vision?

♦ Should particular attention be paid to helping the child develop effective listening skills?

What is important is that the child has access to a visual assessment as early as possible. This is for several reasons (Leat, Shute and Westall 1999):

♦ Some conditions such as retinoblastoma (tumours of the eye) may have the potential to cause blindness or become life-threatening if not treated

♦ There may be threats to the development of binocular vision such as squints and amblyopia

♦ Significant refractive errors such as severe long and short sight may lead to underachievement and difficulties with socialization

♦ Conditions such as cataract prevent a clear retinal image and thus impair the development of visual acuity

Introduction

Fortunately, there is now greater awareness of the importance of the role of vision in learning and this is particularly the case in the early years. Many playthings are based on the principles of early visual development and it is relatively easy to find toys that use bright colours, movement and high contrast to engage the interest of young children. It is also now more common to find young children wearing glasses that have been prescribed following a visual assessment. There is more recognition too of the importance of talking directly to the child and clinicians are more aware of the need to support parents following diagnosis, as illustrated by this response to the RNIB survey 'Shaping The Future' (2001):

> When my daughter was diagnosed as having nystagmus and a form of albinism at six months we were devastated. However, five years down the line we are delighted that her vision though impaired is really quite good. We have great respect and admiration for the medical profession who have looked after us throughout.

As technology comes to play an ever greater role in the lives of young children, there is much more scope for access to information and play activities regardless of the level of vision or visual loss experienced by the child. The role of specialist teachers working with families and children in the early years has also expanded. Peripatetic (itinerant) teachers work for visual impairment services and have received additional training to meet the needs of children who have severe visual impairment or are blind. They are employed in a number of ways, sometimes through local authority

Children's Services or within provision for the early years. They can help by suggesting practical ways for parents and carers to help their children and can offer support at the various transition points in the life of a child. They are able to recommend equipment and to provide materials suitable for a child's level of functional vision. They can also advise on visual stimulation and any environmental adaptations and will assess the functional needs of the child.

A child with a visual impairment has as much right as any other child to ongoing and appropriate support throughout their early years, through education and on into the world of work and leisure.

Part One

Understanding the World – The Senses

1

The Mysterious Case of Vision

We live in an increasingly visual world. Vision provides us with information at the blink of an eye and with as little effort. Yet, this most important sense is highly complex and we still do not fully understand how it works. Most of us give vision little thought – we open our eyes and we see. But one of the strangest things about vision is that we also 'see' in our dreams when our eyes are closed and in our imagination when we read a book or remember a friend. Vision is not simply 'out there' it is also inside our thoughts and imagination. In fact, vision is so integral to our lives and consciousness that we simply take it for granted. It is only when we are confronted with print that is too small to read or a face in a photograph too blurred to identify that we become conscious of our vision at all.

Functional vision

Human sight evolved to give us good access to visual information under normal daylight conditions. We have extended the use of our sight through the introduction of artificial light. By this means we are able to spend longer working at visual tasks. Functional vision is geared to respond to light and movement both in the distance and at close quarters. This gave our hunter–gatherer ancestors the means to hunt from a distance and collect roots and small berries by using their near vision. A visual response to movement allowed us to track the speed and distance of the animals we hunted but we were also able to run to get out of the way of those animals that hunted us. Spatial information was enhanced by our ability to perceive a three-dimensional world. Binocular (3D) vision is made possible because the information from both our separate eyes is integrated and processed by the brain. In modern life these components of vision are not as important to survival, yet for urban dwellers crossing roads is sometimes not unlike escaping a deadly predator. Reaching out to select items in a crowded supermarket can feel very much like hunting and gathering. The fundamentals of sight therefore remain:

♦ Response to light and colour

♦ Response to movement: both our own and the movement around us

The functional components of vision can be summarized as:

♦ Discrimination – is something out there and where is it?

♦ Resolution – what shape is it?

♦ Recognition – what is it?

♦ Understanding – what does it do?

The 'where' and 'what' of vision

In this chapter we are making a distinction between sight and vision. This is an artificial distinction but is helpful when thinking about the eye as a mechanism for transmitting an image and the visual brain as the 'nerve centre' of visual processing. In reality, the eye globe is an extension of the brain itself. One can think of the eye as a sort of outpost concerned with sight, collecting and transmitting images via the optic nerve. These images are then interpreted and assimilated through the process of vision. The development of vision is inextricably linked to other aspects of development. Given this interdependence between vision and our ability to interact with the world around us it is not surprising that a visual loss or impairment can have a significant impact on the developing child. It is therefore particularly important to examine current models of visual development when considering any possible disabilities of sight.

Jeanette Atkinson (2000) offers a comprehensive review of the research into the development of the visual brain. From her work and that of other researchers there is evidence to indicate that there are two key functions of the brain which underpin the development of vision. These are described as the *dorsal* and *ventral* streams. The *dorsal stream* is concerned with action and motor control, such as eye movements and reaching (the 'where' of vision). Response from the dorsal stream is fast, automatic and an unconscious action-based reaction to a stimulus in the environment. The *ventral stream* helps us to develop an understanding of the visual world and build up a memory bank of images for future recognition (the 'what' of vision). Each of these streams has a variety of elements which link to different aspects of development. As our movement and interactions become more refined so our visual understanding of what is happening around us grows in complexity.

How vision works

In order to consider what can go wrong with the visual process it is necessary to begin with the most obvious components in the complex set of relationships which constitute vision. Although it is a massive simplification, it helps to think of the visual system as comprising three parts:

The eyes

The optic nerve

The cerebral cortex

The eyes

Until the late 1700s the eyes were thought to be solely responsible for vision (Jan and Freeman 1998) and they remain the principal organ most people still associate with sight. Much later in the 1900s doctors and researchers working with soldiers who had suffered head injuries identified links between some of these injuries and visual loss. This led to greater emphasis on, and growing interest in, the visual function of the brain. Our eyes are also important because of their role in communication. Establishing eye contact is a vital aspect of communication and socialization.

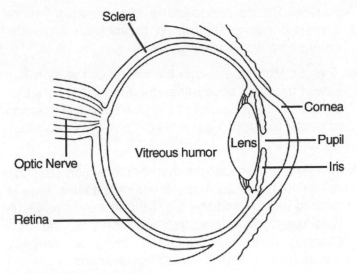

Figure 1. Diagram of the eye

The eyeball is round, with a white, tough outermost layer called the *sclera*. The sclera surrounds the eyeball. The eyeball can be described as having a front (window), middle (globe) and a back.

The front of the eye
The front of the eye contains the equipment necessary for focusing an image onto the back of the eye. In this part of the eye are:

♦ *The cornea* (a transparent protective cover to the front of the eye which acts as a light-bending ('refractive') surface). The cornea is formed from the sclera. Because there are no blood vessels in the cornea, it is normally clear and has a shiny

13

surface. The cornea is extremely sensitive – there are more nerve endings in the cornea than anywhere else in the body.

♦ *The pupil* (the opening in the centre of the iris). The size of the pupil determines the amount of light that enters the eye. Doctors often evaluate the reaction of pupils to light to determine a person's neurological function.

♦ *The lens* (a transparent membrane which changes shape to focus light rays). The crystalline lens is located just behind the iris. Its purpose is to focus light onto the retina. In young people, the lens changes shape to adjust for close or distance vision. This action is called accommodation. With age, the lens gradually hardens, diminishing our ability to accommodate.

♦ *The iris* (the round, coloured part of the eye which adjusts the size of the pupil so that varying amounts of light reaches the lens). The colour, texture and patterns of each person's iris are as unique as a fingerprint.

The middle of the eye (the eye globe)
The front and middle sections of the eye are filled with liquids which maintain an optimum focusing shape and pressure within the eye globe. In the front portion of the eye (the anterior chamber) is a watery substance (*aqueous humor*) that provides oxygen and nutrients to the inside of the cornea and to the lens, and gives the front of the eye its form and shape.

Within the middle of the eye is the *vitreous humor*.

The vitreous is a thick, jelly-like transparent substance that fills the centre of the eye. It is composed mainly of water and comprises about two thirds of the eye's volume. The viscous properties of the vitreous humor allow the eye to return to its normal shape if compressed. In children, the vitreous has a consistency similar to an egg white. With age it gradually thins and becomes more liquid.

The back of the eye
The back of the eye is made up of a thin membrane called the *retina*. The retina contains millions of light-sensitive cells that capture light rays and convert them into electrical impulses. These impulses travel along the optic nerve where they are turned into images in the cerebral cortex. Because of their shapes these cells are known as *rods* and *cones*. Broadly speaking rod cells are responsible for side vision in low light and cones for fine and colour vision in bright light. Cone cells are most densely packed within the *fovea*, the central portion of the *macula* which is the area of most acute vision.

The optic nerve

Connecting to the back of the eye is the optic nerve attached through the *optic disc*. All signals converted by the cells in the retina travel along the optic nerve. Because the eyes are attached separately to the optic nerve the information from each eye has to be integrated in order to produce a single (though upside down) image. The point at which this crossover takes place is called the *optic chiasma*.

The cerebral cortex

The cerebral cortex is where information collected via the optic nerve is finally processed and the image becomes the right way up. The primary visual cortex responds but so do dozens of other visual areas of the cerebral cortex.

Less than five per cent of visually impaired people are totally blind. Most have some level of vision.

Early vision

But what does the anatomy and physiology of vision mean in everyday life? Because the eyes (as part of the brain) develop very early in gestation, the newly born infant is equipped with the components of a sophisticated visual system. At birth, babies can perceive light, turning towards a light source but shutting their eyes if the light is too bright. Babies have been shown to have an innate preference for the human face. Until around the second month areas of high contrast such as the mouth, hairline and eyes seem especially important in capturing the interest of the infant.

After a few days, newly born babies can already discriminate their mother's face from other female faces. These visual abilities help the baby to form a relationship with her carer and lay the foundations for early communication. The world of the baby is a near one, so the visual experience she will receive will be close and impressionistic rather than in sharp focus. Movement is of special interest to the baby. Visual acuity (the ability to see fine detail) and contrast sensitivity (response to the light and dark parts of an image) develop rapidly in the first six months of life and then continue at a steady rate of development until the child is around 5 to 6 years of age when they approximate with those of the adult. So vision is therefore a dynamic process that is integral to the overall development of the child.

Functionally, we can therefore think of visual development as operating at two levels. The first level relates to the early survival needs of the newborn baby. At this level images are large and near and tend to cover the whole of the retina. The baby has very little need for fine discrimination. The ability to respond to movement is important at this stage as the human face, particularly the eyes and mouth, is continually moving while the adult 'looks' and 'speaks'. Babies copy these movements. The ability to attend to facial movement enhances communication between the carer and child.

The second level of visual development takes place as the infant's world enlarges from the close interaction of feeding and is informed through the integration of input from other senses. It is this higher level of vision that enables us to recognize objects and to understand their properties. Visually it becomes more important therefore to have greater visual acuity (finer discrimination of detail in a variety of circumstances). Head control is essential in helping children to direct their gaze, as is the further refinement of eye movements which enable them to scan and track objects. Other sensory feedback is gained as hand–eye coordination is established. Although visual skills go on being

Visual Needs

developed and refined until children are between 8 to 12 years of age, by the time they reach school age at around 5 years, youngsters without any visual impairment have good contrast sensitivity and can:

♦ See in colour

♦ See in depth

♦ Control the movements of their eyes

♦ See in detail

♦ See all round while also attending to an object in central view

An approximate hierarchy of visual skills is:

Level 1

♦ Child responds to light

♦ Child attends to people and movement in close proximity

♦ Side vision is more developed than central vision

♦ Child views part of object rather than whole

♦ Simple and uncrowded visual input is more easily processed

Level 2

♦ Child tracks moving object or light

♦ Child becomes interested in distant objects

♦ Central vision and interest in detail develops

♦ Child is able to view whole object

♦ Child becomes interested in more complex visual information

♦ Child becomes interested in smaller objects

Assessment of vision

In this section the emphasis is on those children who have already been identified as having some sort of visual difficulty. This may have been noticed during routine visits to a child development clinic or may have been identified soon after birth in a hospital setting. The child may have been referred for general health worries and the medical practitioner conducting the physical examination may have noticed something unusual in the child's visual response. A parent or carer may have become concerned. The child is then referred to someone who specializes in the measurement of vision but who can also prescribe medication or possibly surgery (see 'Who's Who' section at the end of the chapter).

Assessment of vision tends to be considered from different perspectives by the various professionals involved. Those from the medical professions will be trying to gain a clinical perspective. They will want to determine whether the child's visual problems are linked to any other more global medical conditions and will also want to find out if the child's condition is stable, deteriorative or likely to improve. They particularly want to know what sort of medical intervention might help the child's vision to improve or stabilize. There is a range of standardized tests, but these need to be adapted to suit the needs of very young children or a child with multiple disabilities. This is because:

♦ Most tests rely on some verbal communication

♦ Most tests rely on a concept of functioning tied to chronological age

♦ Most tests rely on children being physically able to control their environment

Generally speaking, the information received from these assessments will be of some but limited use for the parent or teacher who wants to know about the child's vision in everyday situations. The disadvantage of clinical procedures is that generally they:

♦ Are in unfamiliar environments

♦ Are administered by people who do not know the child

♦ Focus on one aspect of the child

♦ Are inflexible because of pressures of time

Increasingly assessments are becoming more multi-disciplinary and involve parents and a range of professionals such as a specialist teacher of children who are visually impaired. The advantage of the teacher or carer being involved in assessing the child's functional vision is:

♦ The child is with familiar people

♦ The child is in a familiar environment

- Assessment can be linked to everyday activities
- Materials used will be familiar to the child
- Assessment will be at the pace of the child
- Assessment can be linked to visual stimulation

Where does assessment start?

Functional assessment has to be ongoing but basic information should include:

- Medical information
- The clinical assessment provided by the ophthalmologist (if one is available) or other clinician
- Reports on the child's overall progress
- The views of the child
- Parental observations and comments in relation to the home environment
- The general health of the child
- Any medication and possible effects
- Details of any low-vision aids and lighting requirements (if known)
- The preferred viewing angle and viewing distance of the child
- The general movement and posture of the child

Observation is the major tool for gathering information on the child's functioning. Observations need to note the following visual responses:

- How the child responds to light

- How the child's eyes move

- The child's shifting gaze

- The blinking reflex

- The movement of the child's face and if she screws up her face when 'looking'

- The child's response to colour

- Whether the child can track a moving object

Family, nursery and infant school videos are often a helpful source of information. Using video the child can be observed in natural settings over time.

Testing children's vision

Visual acuity

Visual acuity (VA) is the ability to see fine detail both near and at a distance. There are various ways of measuring visual acuity. The commonest way of measuring is by using letter charts.

Letter charts

The Snellen chart is the most famous test used to assess visual acuity. It was developed in 1862. The Snellen chart has a series of letters or numbers, with the largest at the top. As the observer reads down the chart, the letters gradually become smaller. The usual testing distance is 6 metres or 20 feet. Each line of the chart relates to the distance at which a viewer with normal sight could identify the letters on that line. Normal adult visual acuity is therefore 6/6 (20/20). However, if the observer can only read the top line at 6 metres which equates to normal vision at 60 metres then this would be recorded as 6/60 (20/200).

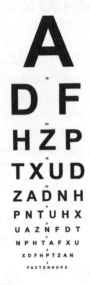

Figure 2. The Snellen Chart

The Tumbling E test
The Snellen letter chart relies on the ability to recognize and communicate the letters seen. However, for those who cannot read the alphabet, there are various other versions. The Tumbling E chart has the capital letter E facing in different directions and the person being tested must determine which direction the E is pointing: up, down, left or right. A similar version is

the Landolt C, where the viewer identifies the gap in the C.

The LogMAR chart designed by Bailey and Lovie
Recently, specialists have advocated the use of an updated version of Snellen to overcome some of its flaws. This chart is called the Bailey–Lovie Acuity Chart and does not record acuity as a Snellen fraction (Leat *et al.*1999), but as the logarithm of the minimum angle of resolution (LogMAR). Originally its use was limited to research, where measuring and monitoring vision has to be very accurate. But this chart is now more widely used. The Bailey–Lovie chart is based on the same principle as the Snellen chart with letters/symbols which decrease in size. However, the change from one line to the next is mathematical and accurately calculated. Each line is 80 per cent of the preceding line and the space between the letters on each line is uniform. Unlike Snellen there are an equal number of letters on each line. The letters chosen are Sloan

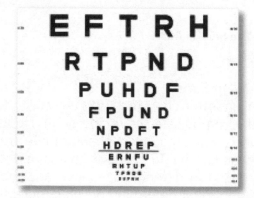

Figure 3. A LogMAR chart

24

letters (i.e. those with equal readability). The uniformity of the chart makes it very useful at any distance, as conversions are easy to do. For example, acuity of 6/6 using this chart would be represented as 0.0 and 6/60 as 1.0. Acuity better than 6/6 has a negative score. So 6/4 equates to −0.176. This greater accuracy is particularly important when we are dealing with a population with less than typical vision.

Snellen/metres	Snellen/feet	LogMAR
6/60	20/200	1.0
6/24	20/70	0.6
6/12	20/40	0.3
6/6	20/20	0

Table 1. *Example of a conversion chart*

Testing visual acuity in very young children or those with limited communication skills requires other acuity tests.

Letter matching tests

Letter or picture matching tests are where the child matches the picture shown by examiners by pointing to it on their card. Children may need to be familiarized with these before testing.

Preferential looking tests such as the Cardiff Acuity Test are a very simple and quick method of acuity assessment. The examiner objectively estimates visual acuity by watching the child's reaction to a stimulus. A pattern or shape of varying size is presented on

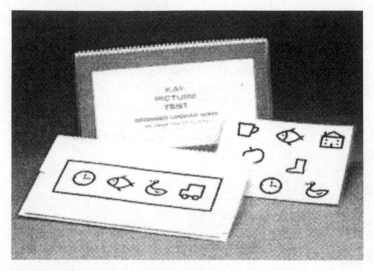

Figure 4. Kay's picture or letter charts

one end of a rectangular card. If the child can see the shape, the eyes will focus on that side of the card. The point where the child can no longer focus and her eyes start to wander is usually the limit of her vision.

Contrast sensitivity

Contrast sensitivity is the ability to discriminate shades of grey. Visual acuity tests are all considered high-contrast tests: they are black letters on a white background. However, the world out there is a world of varying contrasts. To get a better idea of how the child will function in the real world, an assessment of contrast sensitivity provides another piece of the jigsaw, allowing us to form a more complete picture of visual function. Charts like the Pelli–Robson Chart use letters which reduce in contrast (i.e. become fainter). For children there are more exciting tests like *Hiding Heidi*, which uses a picture of a face with different expressions, changing in contrast.

Colour vision

Being able to discern different colours makes it easier for us to function in a colourful world. Colour deficiency is found in people with typical sight. It is more common in males than females: eight per cent of males, compared with less than one per cent of females, have colour-vision defects. Any condition affecting the retinal photoreceptors, particularly cone cells, will affect colour vision.

Children learn to match colours before they learn to name them. Therefore colour-matching tests such as the City tests are very common. Another popular test is the Ishihara test. This test consists of 24 plates with patterns, which can be seen by an observer with typical colour vision but not by those with certain colour deficiencies.

Visual field

Most of the tests already described are mainly about testing central vision. However, to be able to move around safely, good peripheral vision is required. The visual field (also known as the island of vision) is the space around us, which is visible at any one moment.

Any defect of the retina (such as retinitis pigmentosa), of the optic nerve (through glaucoma), or of visual processing (as in cortical visual impairment) can result in reduced visual fields. There are various tests to map the visual field. These range from crude, rudimentary tests to the more sophisticated, computerized type. A simple technique used commonly with babies is to select a toy or other object of interest. The object is moved around from the non-seeing part of the field until a visual response is obtained. This process is repeated in various directions: up, down and from left to right. Children with restricted visual fields may need training to optimize their use of vision.

Depth perception or three-dimensional vision (stereopsis)

Along with being colourful, the world is also three-dimensional (3D). To be able to see three-dimensionally is important when making judgements about depth – for example, reaching for a glass on a table or catching a ball. Tests of stereopsis such as Lang's test are quick and easy to use to determine the presence of 3D vision. The card has hidden shapes and pictures, which can be seen by those with 3D vision. Although the lack of 3D vision may not be such an issue in everyday terms, it may restrict certain activities and occupations such as driving, flying or becoming a surgeon.

Electro-diagnostic tests

All the various tests mentioned above require the child to carry out a task. However, in newly born babies and those children with developmental delay, it may be difficult to get a subjective response. In such cases, objective tests such as electro-diagnostics may be helpful in assessing vision. In these tests electrodes are placed either around the eye (electro-retinogram or ERG) or on the head around the visual cortex (visual evoked potential or VEP). The child is presented with a stimulus such as light, a colour, or a letter. If part of the eye or brain is being used or activated, an electrical signal will be generated. Any disorder of the eye or the visual pathway (the route from the optic nerve to the visual cortex) will reduce or delay the electrical signals.

Visual problems in childhood

There are a number of different types of visual problems experienced by children which include the following:

♦ Loss of acuity resulting in blurred, indistinct vision

♦ Loss of visual field which may affect peripheral (side) or central vision

♦ Over-sensitivity to light

♦ Near or short-sightedness

♦ Colour confusion (sometimes wrongly described as colour blindness)

♦ Visual processing difficulties

Visual problems can be caused by a variety of factors. There may be developmental anomalies that can lead to poor function in a part of the visual system.

Some components of the system may be malformed or incomplete. There may be damage which has been caused as a complication arising from childhood illness. Whatever the reason, children are unlikely to be aware that they have a problem with their vision.

Children with reduced vision should all have full eye examinations. In most cases their visual difficulty may be due to refractive errors and can easily be corrected optically by lenses in a pair of glasses. A refractive error is the inability of the eye to focus sharply on an object. *Refraction* is the process by which optometrists or ophthalmologists will work out the type and strength of corrective lenses required. A special torchlight is shone at the back of the eye. Because the retina is a reflective surface the light bounces back. The movement of this reflected light is used to ascertain the refractive error. This objective test is called *retinoscopy*. In very young children, eye drops to temporarily relax the active focusing muscles may be required before carrying out a retinoscopy. This is known as *cycloplegic refraction* and makes the refraction process more accurate.

The drops cause the pupils to dilate, making the child sensitive to bright sunlight and giving blurred vision. The effects are temporary and last from one to three days. A small percentage of children are allergic to these drops. Parents should consult the eye specialist if redness or soreness occurs or if the effects do not wear off after the given time.

A refractive anomaly occurs when an image falls short of or is projected beyond the retina. Many of us experience the conditions of long or short sight. Although in themselves these conditions are easily improved by the use of lenses, these need to be pre-scribed as soon as possible. Early detection and correc-tion of refractive errors is very important to enable the visual system to develop fully. Uncorrected, these errors may result in amblyopia or 'lazy eye'. Problems with near and distance vision can compound children's difficulties in play and early learning. Refractive anom-alies may occur alone or in combination with other visual impairments such as cortical visual impairment.

There are three types of refractive errors: myopia, hyperopia and astigmatism.

Short sight (myopia)

Children with short sight will experience particular dif-ficulties when visual tasks are presented at a distance. The distance at which the difficulty occurs will depend on the severity of the short sight as well as the type of visual task and the available lighting. The abnormal length of the eyeball, which leads to the image falling short of the retina, causes short sight. Children will not be aware they have this condition and since some children will not yet be verbalizing, careful observation combined with clinical assessment are likely to be the only ways of determining whether lenses will help. For very young children the effects could be:

♦ A lack of interest in their surroundings

♦ Delay or disruption to the development of motor skills because the child cannot see sufficiently to copy the movement of others

♦ An additional impairment to hand–eye coordination

Visual Needs

In many cases myopia runs in the family and some-times gets worse with age, but in most cases stabilizes when the body as well as the eye stops growing. However, there are a very small number of cases where the myopia continues to progress leading to a condition called *pathological myopia* or high-degree myopia.

Once short sight has been diagnosed lenses will be prescribed. Some children who are reluctant to use spectacles may be given contact lenses, though these will usually only be recommended if the child is able to manage them. In both cases the care and monitoring of the lenses is important because dirty or inappropri-ate lenses can make the child's vision less effective and may produce discomfort. Contact lenses can be difficult to fit so parents and staff will need training in their maintenance. Children sometimes resist wearing glasses. The reasons may include:

♦ The heavy, thick lenses may be uncomfortable

♦ The child may need more time to get used to lenses

♦ Children may be visually confused by the seeming change in their environment

♦ The lenses may not be appropriate for the task

Always make sure you know why lenses have been prescribed and for what tasks they are most suitable. Check the fit of glasses and where possible involve children in the care of their lenses.

Long sight (hyperopia)

In long sight the length of the eyeball is too short and the image falls behind the retina. Children will bring objects close to their eyes as their eyes try to *accommodate* to focus on the object. The normal default setting for the eye is distance vision but the lens can be 'squeezed' by its controlling muscle (ciliary muscle). This enables greater magnification of the image for close tasks. The function of accommodation is greatest in children and young adults, and is gradually lost as the lens loses its elasticity with age (from around 40 years). If a child has a squint it may be more noticeable when the child is attempting to look at something near. The effort involved in using vision for close tasks may cause the child considerable discomfort and may shorten an already short attention span. Most children, however, are born with mild hyperopia, which corrects itself without glasses as the child gets older. For ongoing hyperopia, lenses will be prescribed and should be used for all visually near tasks.

Astigmatism

Astigmatism is another common vision problem which may accompany myopia or hyperopia. It is caused if the cornea (the clear window at the front of the eye) has an irregular curvature. Astigmatism can be corrected with optical lenses just as myopia and hyperopia can. Uncorrected astigmatism can cause distorted vision, eyestrain and headaches.

Strabismus (squint)

Strabismus, or squint, occurs when there is a fault in one or more of the eye muscles. This can cause a misalignment leading to 'crossed eye'. There are a variety of different sorts of squints. The child's eyes may turn inwards or may seem to rove in different directions. If the turning eye looks in, it is called *esotropia* or 'convergent squint', and if it looks out it is called *exotropia* or 'divergent squint'. A convergent squint can also occur if the child has one eye that is much more long-sighted than the other, causing it to over-focus.

Squints should be dealt with long before the child reaches school. In untreated children the brain itself will suppress the confusing visual information it is receiving. The child will develop an amblyopic or 'lazy' eye. Even when treated some children never develop good binocular vision. In extreme cases the effects on the child can be:

♦ Poor hand–eye coordination

♦ Problems with scanning

♦ General problems involving close work

♦ Fatigue leading to lack of interest in visual tasks

Amblyopia (lazy eye)

For the visual pathway to develop normally, it requires a clear image from both eyes. If, for some reason, one image is different (as with 'strabismus') or unfocused (as in high hyperopia), the brain will have difficulty fusing the two images to give a single three-dimensional image. Problems with joining the two images may result in double vision. To avoid this, the brain 'switches off' the affected eye causing it to be underdeveloped. Lazy eyes must be treated as soon as possible, by surgery or glasses and then by wearing a patch. By patching the good eye for a set period of time, the lazy eye is forced to work and thus hopefully its visual function is enhanced.

Colour-vision defects

Most colour-vision defects (often incorrectly called colour blindness) are hereditary and present at birth. In mild cases colour-vision defects may cause confusion between different shades of colours such as red and brown. Colour confusion may not cause problems in everyday life but very young children affected by colour confusion can have difficulties learning to name colours and to sort by colour. This can sometimes be thought of as a learning difficulty if staff are unaware of the child's visual problem. In later life there are certain professions where colour confusion can be a barrier to employment. Owing to its genetic nature, more men are affected than women.

Some eye conditions affecting the retina or the optic nerve can result in severe colour-vision defects, i.e. when the light-sensitive cells of the retina do not respond to light and colour as they should do. A rare condition called *achromatopsia*, where cone cells are absent from the retina, causes complete colour blindness.

Visual field loss

Some children, especially those with multiple disabilities, may have a restricted field of vision. Damage or developmental anomalies could have occurred inside the eye globe or the child may have suffered some visual disturbance as in conditions like *hemianopia*. In hemianopia there is a loss of vision in half the visual field. It is important to ask for information on a child's visual field and to observe the child. You may for instance notice the child holds her head at an unusual angle when 'looking'. If the child is also physically disabled and has limited motor control, observations will have to take into account that a child's field loss may be compounded by her postural inclination. What difference does a field loss make?

- ◆ Children will not be motivated to reach for objects presented from their 'blind' side

- ◆ Parts of information can be lost and the child may miss cues

- ◆ The child's overall functional vision will not be stimulated

- ◆ Eating and drinking may be affected because food and drink have not been presented within the child's view

- ◆ In hemianopia there may be problems scanning (particularly if the left side of the visual field is affected), so learning to read could be more difficult

Causes of visual impairment

Around 1.5 million children are blind worldwide, most of these in Africa and Asia.

The causes of visual impairment are not straightforward and can result from any of these factors:

♦ Genetic or hereditary illness

♦ Damage to the eye before, or during, or soon after birth

♦ Damage caused during the early years

A classic example is childhood cataracts. Although cataracts mainly affect older people, they are also one of the causes of childhood visual impairment.

Examples of some common eye conditions causing visual impairment in children are listed below in alphabetical order.

Albinism

This is a name given to a group of inherited conditions. People with albinism have little or no light-absorbing pigment (*melanin*). There are two types: *oculocutaneous* which causes pale skin and pale hair, and *ocular albinism*, which only affects the eye. Although the reason is not yet fully understood, it appears that the lack of melanin affects the development of the fovea (the area of most acute vision) and so visual acuity is reduced. The lack of pigmentation also means that there is an excess of light entering the eye. Albinism can have a number of associated features:

♦ Roving eye movements (nystagmus)

♦ Strabismus

♦ Photophobia (avoidance of light because of discomfort)

♦ Short and long sight

♦ Astigmatism

Most children with albinism cope well but may need access to large print and materials using high contrast.

Cataracts

A cataract is an eye condition when the normally transparent lens of the eye is not clear. This affects the way light enters and focuses on the retina causing reduced vision and in some case blindness. Childhood cataracts can be a result of infection in the womb, poor maternal and child health, or can be due to an accident affecting the eye. Many congenital cataracts are inherited. Cataracts can be treated effectively by surgically removing the unclear lens and replacing it with a clear artificial lens, or glasses and contact lenses. Cataracts must be detected and treated as soon as possible to avoid amblyopia.

The level of visual impairment will depend on the density and position of the cataracts. Most children will have problems with both near and distance vision. Cataracts also cause scattering of light; therefore many children will be light sensitive. Early intervention is vital for children with congenital cataracts. Such obstructions to light must be eliminated to allow normal visual development.

The child's affected lens or lenses will be removed and artificial lenses prescribed. It is worth remembering that when cataracts are present the child will be:

♦ Sensitive to light

♦ Unable to see clearly

♦ Possibly affected by additional complications such as nystagmus and squints

♦ Experiencing difficulties in low lighting conditions

Coloboma

When one part of the eye or more does not develop fully in the womb, this leaves a cleft or 'coloboma'. This developmental anomaly can affect the iris, lens, retina and the optic nerve head. Coloboma may be inherited; however, most occur just by chance. The level of vision will depend on the site and extent of damage. One or both eyes may be affected. Microphthalmos, where the eye is abnormally small and anophthalmos, where the eye has completely failed to develop, are extreme types of coloboma.

Cortical visual impairment (CVI)

CVI is one of the largest causes of childhood blindness in the UK and other parts of the developed world.

Visual Needs

A growing percentage of children considered to have a congenital visual impairment are likely to have additional needs. This is largely a result of extreme prematurity combined with a very low birth-weight. In the past such pre-term babies would not have survived, but with greater advances in medical science there is much that can be done to help these tiny infants. While many will go on to develop typically, some will require ongoing medical attention and life support, and will have a range of disabilities. It is these multiply disabled infants who are also likely to have difficulty in processing visual information. This is described as cortical visual impairment or cerebral visual disturbance (CVD). The visual loss will vary depending on the cause and site of the damage along the visual pathway. This loss can range from mild and subtle effects to more complex, and even complete, absence of visual function.

Some multiply disabled children will have damage to the visual pathways from the retina. This damage can occur at any point in the pathways or in the cerebral cortex itself. Damage may take place before or after birth. It can be caused by genetic or other factors such as anoxia (lack of oxygen), infection, head injury or developmental anomalies in the brain. It is rare that children affected in this way have no residual vision. In the vast majority of cases other types of disability, particularly physical disability, will accompany problems processing visual information. Because of the importance of vision as a primary source of information, anything that can be done to stimulate visual development in cortically visually impaired children is likely to also assist other aspects of their development.

The eyes of children with CVI appear normal so there is often an initial difficulty in recognizing their visual loss. The additional communication and motor impairments of these multiply disabled children may further mask their visual needs. From observations made by parents, carers and teachers, as well as clinicians such as Groenveld (1993), certain characteristics of CVD have been identified:

◆ Normal healthy appearance of eyes
◆ Highly variable visual performance
◆ Short visual attention span
◆ Fascination with light
◆ Tendency to hold objects close to view
◆ Peripheral field loss

It is difficult to identify any one factor affecting the functioning of children who have a cortical visual impairment but their overall level of functioning tends to decrease when they are:

◆ In unfamiliar environments
◆ Tired
◆ Lacking in energy (using their vision takes more energy for cortically visually impaired children)
◆ In poor health

These factors will also influence their visual performance but particular regard will need to be paid to:

Visual Needs

♦ The amount of available light (especially task lighting)
♦ The visual environment
♦ The effects of medication

In many ways the needs of cortically visually impaired children are similar to the needs of children at the early levels of visual maturation. Difficulties exist for the child when presented with complicated visual information. They will tend to hold objects close to their eyes to fill their visual field with one object at a time. They find it easier if objects are placed apart and will more readily engage visually if an additional light source is provided. Fatigue is common and it would seem that these children need more energy to process visual information. Certain colours seem to attract their attention particularly and, when they are mobile, they are able to navigate their environment well, although some children seem unable to recognize objects within it.

What can be done to help these children access visual information?

♦ Provide plenty of light and contrast to enhance visual activities
♦ Stimulate the visual interest of the child by the use of bold geometric patterns with good contrast
♦ Back up visual information with additional information for the other senses
♦ Use primary colours and keep colours and objects linked so the child will associate them (for example, always a yellow mug for lunchtime)

◆ Present visual information in short bursts and in a simple form

◆ Give children as much control over their environment as possible

◆ Use refractive paper and stickers to draw the child's attention to objects

◆ Draw the child's attention to their own movements by giving them brightly coloured socks or gloves

Glaucoma

Glaucoma is a common condition affecting two per cent of the adult population in the UK. The optic nerve at the back of the eye is damaged, usually due to increased pressure in the eye. The eye is normally full of a fluid (aqueous humor), which provides nutrition to the eye. This is continually being made and drained. Often there is damage to the drainage system, which causes a buildup of pressure. Congenital glaucoma occurs either at birth or soon after. It can affect one or both eyes. The treatment involves drainage surgery to relieve the pressure and avoid further damage. The visual loss varies depending on the extent of the damage to the eye. It may lead to reduced peripheral vision, also known as 'tunnel vision' and even blindness if left untreated.

Nystagmus

In nystagmus the child's eyes seem to move constantly (oscillate). This condition is sometimes called 'dancing eyes'. The child has no control over this movement. Nystagmus may occur alone but more commonly it appears in combination with other conditions such as albinism. If the child has good general motor control she may turn her head and find the 'null' point in her nystagmus where the effects of the oscillation is minimized. Children with physical disabilities will need help to try a range of head positions to maximize their vision.

Optic nerve disorders

There are a number of disorders of the optic nerve. Some are as a result of developmental anomalies such as *optic nerve hypoplasia*, or as a result of progressive damage as in the case of glaucoma. The amount of vision retained will vary according to the extent and location of the disorder and the nature of the anomaly.

Retinopathy of prematurity (ROP)

Retinopathy of prematurity normally affects small, premature babies in incubation units. The condition is caused by the growth of abnormal retinal blood vessels as a result of extra oxygen in the body from the incubator. These new blood vessels are fragile and start to leak and cause scarring. In some cases this can lead to retinal detachment. ROP can be treated effectively if caught early enough. In the UK, all premature babies are screened for ROP. Abnormal blood vessels are destroyed either by burning (*laser treatment*) or freezing (*cryotherapy*). The treatment will control damage, but most children will have some degree of visual loss and may also be highly myopic or hyperopic.

Retinitis pigmentosa (RP)

Retinitis pigmentosa is the name given to a group of inherited disorders of the retina, particularly the light-sensitive cells (rods and cones). RP usually develops during the first or second decade of life. First, there is a loss of peripheral vision and the ability to see in dim light (night blindness). A degree of central vision is retained. The term 'tunnel' vision is sometimes used to describe the effects of RP. Later, in some cases, the condition can progress to severe visual impairment and blindness. Currently, there is no medical cure for this condition. RP is often associated with other conditions and syndromes. Children with RP will need to be helped to maximize the use of their field of vision and will need training in mobility to overcome both their visual field difficulties and their night blindness.

Who's Who in vision health and care?

A child's eye problems may be identified at birth by the paediatrician (child specialist), by a general practitioner (GP) or the health visitor. Later, families and schools may become aware of problems with sight by observing the behaviour of the child. Once detected, the problem has to be assessed fully by specialists who deal with eyes. There are several professionals who may be involved in the care of a child with visual impairment.

Ophthalmologists

Ophthalmologists are medical doctors who specialize in eyes. They detect and treat eye conditions. They are qualified to carry out surgery. Some specialize further to become children's eye specialists: paediatric ophthalmologists.

Ophthalmic nurses

They are nurses who specialize in eyes, working alongside ophthalmologists in eye clinics, operating theatres and wards.

Orthoptists

Orthoptists work with ophthalmologists. They are involved with patients who have eye-muscle problems such as squints, double vision and amblyopia prior to treatment, and are then involved in monitoring the treatment's success.

Optometrists

Historically known as ophthalmic opticians, optometrists are trained professionals who examine eyes, prescribe and fit glasses or contact lenses. They also detect eye disease and refer when necessary.

Opticians

Also known as 'dispensing opticians.' They fit and supply the most appropriate spectacles after taking account of each patient's lifestyle and vocational needs. They are also able to fit contact lenses after undergoing further specialist training.

Low-vision practitioners

These can be any of the above professionals, but most are optometrists, who carry out a thorough assessment of the visual loss and make suggestions as to how to enhance a child's remaining vision. They can prescribe devices, also known as low-vision aids such as magnifiers, telescopes and CCTVs.

Summary

In this chapter we have discussed some of the main features of vision and some common forms of visual problems. There is much we still do not know about the visual process even though the mechanics of sight have been understood for many years. It is worth stressing the following:

◆ Vision evolves over a long period – it typically takes around five years and sometimes longer for children's vision to develop fully

◆ The environment is key to how well we can use the vision we have – good lighting without glare is essential

◆ We need to give babies and young children things to look at which interest them

◆ Vision is part of a whole sensory and physical experience and does not operate in isolation

Visual Needs

To conclude: the effective use of vision relies on a combination of factors:

Physical

♦ A clear image being conveyed from the front of the eye to the retina

♦ Neural pathways transmitting the image to the visual cortex

♦ Effective neural connections transmitting visual information to the relevant centres in the brain

Perceptual/Cognitive

♦ The link between the physical exploration of objects and an understanding of their shape, density and texture

♦ Experience

♦ Memory

♦ Understanding

2

Sound Track

Introduction

For children growing up with little or no vision, hearing can assume a greater-than-usual importance in the way that they perceive, understand and engage with the world and, crucially, in the way that they interrelate with other people. Indeed, from an adult perspective, many blind and partially sighted people themselves recognize the central function that hearing has played and continues to play in their lives (Goldstein 1999). However, it is not the case that hearing merely substitutes seeing as a source of information about what is going on and the nature and whereabouts of people and objects in the immediate environment. Most of us interpret our surroundings through a synthesis of sensory information in which vision takes the lead, coordinating and making sense of other input. Hence, supporting children with visual impairment in the development of their listening skills is at once important and challenging.

With this in mind, we will consider how hearing typically develops, as well as the likely impact of visual loss on that development. We will discuss strategies for encouraging the functionality of hearing to evolve, and how these may support areas of cognitive development that visual loss can potentially impede. Most importantly, we will suggest ways in which sound, and in particular music, can be a source of pleasure and sheer fun to children – unique in its capacity for enhancing the quality of life.

The development of hearing

Hearing starts to develop early on – typically, four to three months before birth – and by the time they are born, babies are likely to be particularly sensitive to sounds with which they have become familiar in the womb, and prefer them to others: their mother's voice, for example, the language she speaks and pieces of music to which she has had significant exposure (Lecanuet 1996). The structures of the inner ear appear to be mature at birth, and the abilities of infants to perceive pitch (the 'high' or 'low' of sound), timbre (its 'tone colour') and loudness are similar to those of adults – better, in fact, at high frequencies (Fassbender 1996). So, while there is a gradual improvement in auditory sensitivity until the age of ten, what really matters for parents and carers of blind and partially sighted children whose hearing is not severely impaired is the *functional* development of sound processing. What is the significance of particular sounds: what do they mean and how do they affect the child concerned?

William Gaver (1993) suggests that there are essentially two ways in which we hear sounds: through 'musical listening', which focuses on *perceptual qualities* such as pitch and loudness, and via 'everyday listening' which is concerned with attending to *events* such as a dog barking or a car driving by. To these two categories we should add the perception and cognition of speech sounds which, research indicates, are processed through dedicated neurological pathways (Thurman and Welch 2000). This means that, in Western cultures at least, sound fulfils three main functions which, we may assume, become gradually more delineated during the early years until, by school age, they are readily distinguishable. This thinking is illustrated in Figure 5 on page 52.

Of course, in real life, things are not as neat and tidy as this, and the three types of sound function may well be mixed up together: think of a child in a supermarket, for example, who is being assailed simultaneously by background music (ultimately intended to encourage shoppers to spend more), her father discussing the price of baked beans with a friend and the clatter of tins on the shelf. Then, two sound functions may consciously be combined, as in songs (the fusion of music and speech), or a single sound may serve a dual or even triple function, as is the case with clock chimes (comprising musical, everyday sounds which also convey symbolic meaning).

Amazingly, learning to make sense of all these different types of auditory input – developing different ways of processing sounds according to their context and function – usually occurs without specially thought-through intervention on the part of parents or carers. However, as we shall see, much of the information that assists a child initially to distinguish the different functions that sound can fulfil, and making sense of each, comes through vision. Hence there is a danger that infants with severe visual impairment, particularly

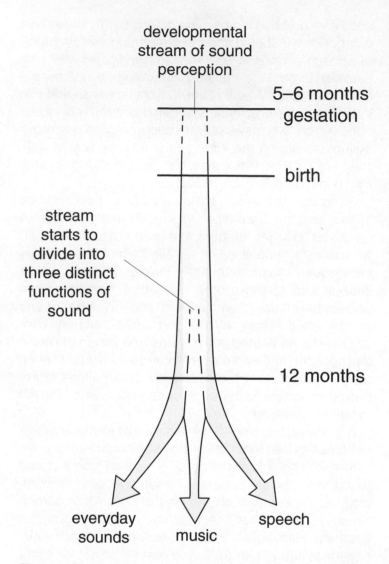

Figure 5. The development of functional sound processing in the early years

those with learning difficulties, may take longer to make sense of things in auditory terms, and that much of the world around will remain a confusing place for them well into childhood and beyond. But there is a lot that can be done in order to mitigate this risk, and as a first step it will be helpful to know more about the differences in the way that the brain handles everyday sounds, speech and music.

The three functions of sound

Everyday sounds

Just by watching, children normally learn that one set of sounds in the environment is variously connected with particular things, events, places or people. These sounds derive from the physical world through contingent or causal relationships: for example, the door closing makes a distinct 'click' (or occasionally more of a bang!), the vacuum cleaner produces a loud, continuous hum, and a range of fascinating sounds emanate from the family car. Once the connection between sound and object is known, the former can be used to identify the latter. So a child will recognize the vacuum cleaner being operated in the next room, for example, without needing to see it.

Speech

Similarly, spoken words can be indicative of things, events, places and people, but they can also represent abstract concepts such as feelings. This is because the sounds that make up words are typically linked to their referent only through association – and so quite arbitrarily – having no particular auditory connection with that which is represented. Hence the very different sound-patterns 'bird', *oiseau*, *Vogel* and *uccello*, for instance, can all mean the same thing in English, French, German and Italian respectively. Again, at first, the necessary associative links are typically learnt through simultaneous exposure in the visual and auditory domains – by seeing something and hearing someone making a distinct utterance that refers to it at the same time.

For sure, the power and subtlety of mature human language means that, for the growing infant, things soon get a lot more complicated than this. Some parts of speech that are needed to qualify concepts or describe the relationships between them do not correspond to anything tangible in the physical world. (For example, as I write this, my two year old and another child are playing in the sandpit, wrestling over a bucket and spade, both shouting 'mine!', and each entirely clear about what the other means.) Furthermore, a great deal of language (and the thinking that it represents) is reliant on metaphor, whereby one thing is conceived in terms of another (Fauconnier 1994). Nonetheless, for most children, seeing in everyday situations catalyses the development of language: it provides the subject of shared attention, giving a reason to attend to what people are saying (and, in turn, to speak). Seeing, too, is essential to making sense of what is heard: speech is meaningful and relevant to children since it relates to entities and events that they have observed in the real world, and the relationships that they have inferred between them.

The *emotional* content of vocal communication, however, appears to be less reliant on vision. For example, one study found that primary-aged school-children, blind since birth, were just as accurate as their fully sighted counterparts at recognizing vocally expressed emotion (Minter, Hobson and Pring 1991). Similarly, at a later stage in development, the *aesthetic* aspect of spoken language, including the sounding qualities of words and their juxtaposition (expressed, for example, through rhyme and alliteration) are learnt and appreciated without the need for visual input.

Music

Music, in pure form (without accompanying words or actions), engages the most abstract of the three streams of auditory function. Indeed, music's place in early human survival is a matter of some contention; its evolutionary purpose remains unclear (Cross 2003). Unlike everyday sounds, music does not derive its meaning from direct links with the environment, and, unlike speech, it does not rely on connections made through association. So how and what does it communicate?

Since music need not refer to anything beyond itself, its architecture is necessarily 'self-referencing', whereby its constituent sounds are felt (usually non-consciously) to derive from one another – or, conversely, to generate each other – through imitation. As a piece unfolds in time, its sounds appear to copy some of those that precede, and it is this repetition that brings a sense of order to music, that makes it coherent to listeners (Ockelford 2004a). Generally speaking,

the greater the degree of replication, the more immediate the comprehensibility. So pop songs, for
example, which are engineered to be assimilated by
their listeners straight away, are replete with material
that is heard over and over again: just consider how
often the main theme – the 'hook' – of a song is heard
in its three or four minutes of playing time. Whatever
the style involved, the intrinsically imitative nature of
music means that to make sense of it in structural
terms, which is dependent on our capacity to process
abstract patterns of sound, vision is not needed at all.

But what of musical enjoyment? Like speech, music
has an affective component, and it is this that most
people find attractive: it is not our ability to recognize
the internal logic of musical structures that sells CDs
and downloads in their millions each week, but music's
power to engage listeners on an emotional level.
Whether a piece makes them happy or sad, dreamy or
aroused, people enjoy being moved by abstract patterns of sound. How does this work, and what part
does vision typically play? There are a number of theories of how music conveys emotion (Juslin and Sloboda
2001). My own model (Ockelford 2004b) builds on the
intuition that all musical sounds and the relationships
between them potentially bear affect, a characteristic
that appears to arise from two sources. One is the
capacity of the general features of sound (high/low,
loud/soft, quick/slow, and so on) to induce emotion,
which may ultimately stem from features of maternal
vocalization (Malloch 1999/2000). The other is the
music-specific qualities of the sounds that are used in
most genres, which are similarly capable of inducing a
consistent emotional response, within and sometimes

between cultures (Scherer, Banse and Wallbott 2001). For example, in the Western tradition of the last four centuries or so, the 'major' key is often associated with happiness (as in the familiar wedding march by Mendelssohn, for instance) and the 'minor' key with sadness (as in the well-known funeral march by Chopin). But how are these capacities of sound manipulated to ensure that music offers a unified and coherent aesthetic experience over time? Just as one feature of a piece is felt to derive structurally from another through imitation, so too are their related affective responses and, since the discrete emotional impacts of successive notes, chords and themes are linked through a sense of derivation (whereby the response to one sound is felt to generate another or others), a kind of abstract narrative is built up over time – rather like a story that is devoid of concrete meaning. For sure, this intrinsically musical response may be linked, directly or indirectly, with other sensory information. But, to the extent that music is the art of combining sounds for their own sake, it requires no visual input. Hence it is unique among the three functions of sound identified above.

Strategies for minimizing the impact of visual impairment on processing sound

Everyday sounds

There are a number of ways in which vision typically informs, coordinates and even directs the perception of everyday sounds. From early in post-natal development, for example, sight makes the link between much auditory information and its sources or causes in the physical environment. Vision answers key questions such as 'who or what is making that noise?', 'how?' and 'where is it coming from?'. Most everyday situations are characterized by several sounds jostling for attention at the same time, and since we cannot concentrate on them all, prioritization is necessary. Often, without our being aware of it, our hearing is directed to our primary visual interest of the moment, with other auditory input automatically suppressed to avoid cognitive overload. This means that the principal sound to which we are attending is made to seem louder than the others around. We will even ascribe a sound to a visual image when its source is actually elsewhere (particularly noticeable in the cinema, for example). Above all, seeing something or someone can provide the motivation to listen. It may be, for example, a mother's face in close proximity to her baby that directs his attention to her voice, a reverberating cymbal glistening in the light that attunes a child's ears to its shimmering sound, or a toy steam train racing around the track whose electronic chuffing fires the aural imagination of its young owner. In each case, visual images stimulate and sustain attention to sound.

So what can be done to support babies and young children who are blind or partially sighted in developing their listening skills? The very first thing to offer them is your own voice. There is nothing more appealing to babies' ears, and instinctively parents and carers adjust their vocal production to suit their children's still-evolving auditory senses, using a higher pitch-range than normal, for instance, and employing a sing-song style of speech in which expressive contours are exaggerated and words are articulated slowly, repeated often and combined with other non-speech sounds. When interacting with a child who is visually impaired, aim to capture these intuitive approaches, exploit them and expand upon them. Use vocalization to substitute for the visual reassurance a baby would otherwise have through seeing you without the need for constant physical contact (Sonksen and Stiff 1999).

Three-month-old baby Amelia has no sight, and her mother Jayne uses her voice in a number of ways to compensate for their lack of visual contact. For example, she tells Amelia when she is about to touch her or pick her up by talking to her gently and telling her what she is going to do. Although Amelia does not understand the words, she is comforted by the reassuring tone of her mother's familiar voice and anticipates that something is about to happen. Jayne also provides an unobtrusive commentary for Amelia as she changes her, bathes her and feeds her, explaining in a natural way what she is doing. Amelia loves this continuous auditory contact – it helps her feel safe and secure – and she coos happily in response. When Jayne cuddles Amelia she sings to her, often using the tunes of nursery rhymes but personalizing the words. Amelia can feel Jayne's breath on her face, hear her voice and feel it resonating through her body as her mother holds her close. She lies quite still in rapt attention: Jayne knows that she is listening and gives her a loving squeeze.

From this restricted, intimate world, parents and carers should seek to broaden children's aural horizons without overextending them, weaning them gradually onto a rich and varied diet of auditory experiences. Parents can start with their own interests and consider whether their child would benefit from sharing in them. Maybe he or she would relish the roar of the crowd at a football match, for instance, the sound of birds in full song, the crash of waves on the beach or the revving of engines at a car rally (Harrison and Crow 1993). In addition, as we shall see, music, the art of organized sound, can play an especially important part in the development of listening skills. Whatever the nature of the sounds concerned, try to encounter the world anew through the ears of the child, being imaginative but systematic in your choice of stimuli and noting particularly those things that cause excitement or give pleasure. Think too about the environments in which sounds are heard: some children love to explore places that echo (caves and large buildings, for example), while others may be intrigued by the way that their voice seems to disappear into nothing at the top of a hill. Children need to learn that the same people or things can sound very different depending on the acoustic qualities of the surroundings in which they are heard (Zimmermann 1997), rather as an object changes in appearance according to the light in which it is seen.

Virtually all objects and events have multisensory potential, and, if it is feasible, support children in experiencing them holistically, using any vision they may have, as well as hearing, touch, smell and taste (Lowenfeld 1974). Encourage them not just to listen to things passively, but to engage with them functionally wherever possible. Young children may be interested in helping to load the washing machine, for example, assist in adding the detergent, close the door with a click, press the right buttons, listen to the rush of water entering and then feel (as well as hear) the vibrations as the cycle progresses. In this way, the fragmented auditory experiences that vision usually integrates can be brought together to form coherent concepts. Gradually, the children will learn what things make which sounds and how. They will come to realize that sound can be a useful indicator of cause and effect.

Bear in mind, though, that vision is often useful in enabling people to predict the sounds that are about to occur (seeing a stick raised above a drum, for example), and, almost inevitably, children with visual impairments will be startled by the unexpected more often than their fully sighted peers. Wherever possible, warn them when sudden sounds are likely, and introduce them to especially noisy environments with care. If possible, let *them* make the sounds first (banging the drum, for example) so that they become accustomed to what is going on in situations where they have control. Over time, through being introduced to a wide range of listening experiences, children with little or no sight may come to tolerate, and hopefully enjoy, an increasing range of noisy sounds. Indeed, sounds of all types may become the principal means of establishing and maintaining their attention.

As well as learning about the real world in day-to-day situations with the help of empathetic adults selecting sounds for them that are salient, blind or partially sighted youngsters may need special opportunities for developing their listening skills in an environment which is devoid of 'auditory clutter' – a small, quiet room, for example, with minimal extraneous noise (Best 1992). Here, it will be easier for children to focus on interacting with just one or two adults, perhaps with some especially chosen objects, to explore their sound-making and other properties thoroughly, and, through sound, to learn to locate them in relation to their own bodies and other sound-makers (Warren 1984). Everyday items have as much potential interest as any others, and in the early stages of development may include, for example, crinkly paper, rattly containers, pots and pans, lengths of chain, and trays of pebbles and shells. Suspending some objects will make them more resonant and easier to relocate once they have been initially explored and discarded. To maximize the effectiveness of learning, the golden rule is to ensure that activities are fun! And it is vital to give young children the space and time to allow them to initiate their own play and to make their own discoveries. Particularly for those who cannot see at all, it is important to strike an appropriate balance between guided activity and self-directed exploration (Nielsen 1992).

Once the development of everyday auditory perception is underway, it can be used to support other areas of learning and a child's evolving independence. For instance, young people's mobility and orientation skills will advance through their increasing ability to derive information from sounds in and the acoustic properties of different environments. Congenitally blind children in particular may develop the skill of 'echolocation', whereby the distances to objects and, to some extent, their physical properties are ascertained by the way sounds reflect off them. Quite intuitively, some children may use vocalizations such as 'clicks' and other sounds to gauge something of the nature of their immediate environment.

Language

Just as the knowledge and understanding of many everyday concepts are usually acquired through vision, so (as we noted above) is the language associated with them. Therefore it is important for parents and carers to ensure that they use sufficient and appropriate language to label, describe and explain to blind and partially sighted children what is around them and what is going on. Similarly, a reasonable proportion of everyday conversation should pertain to things that the children have either encountered directly or can extrapolate from first-hand experience (Webster and Roe 1998).

> Aaron is 4, and does not have enough sight to see images on television or pictures in books. In his reception class, the children are finding out about animals and the countryside, and the teacher is holding up a poster of a fox and discussing this with the group. The teacher knows that Aaron's family have a pet dog, and, by using descriptive language carefully to draw a comparison between this and the fox, Aaron's teacher ensures that he gains a good initial idea of what foxes are like. Later, this information will be reinforced by a visit to a local natural history museum, when Aaron will be able to feel a stuffed fox for himself.

There is some debate as to whether a stream of language accompanying activities may interfere with children's learning, in the belief that it may be difficult for them to focus on linguistic and sensory input at the same time. Clearly, a judgement needs to be made on the part of the adult who is guiding or facilitating things: while it is important not to overwhelm children with excessive description or instruction, neither should they be left in a communicative vacuum (see the case of Amelia above), and both language-assisted and language-free modes of learning may be important at different times. Similarly, the view has been expressed that one should avoid making reference to concepts that a child has not experienced or may not be able to sense directly, such as colour. This is generally felt to be an unnecessary and unhelpful restriction, however: after all, the language to which every young person is typically exposed contains information which he or she only imperfectly understands. The important thing, particularly for children with no sight, is not to *assume* comprehension on their part, and to ensure that they have plenty of opportunities to test and if necessary improve their developing conceptual and linguistic competence.

If insufficient connections are forged between language and the world it is intended to represent, then children's linguistic development may be adversely affected (Wills 1978). Characteristics of speech that have been observed to be unusually prominent in blind children include the confusion of pronouns, 'verbalism' (using words without understanding what they mean) and 'echolalia' (the apparently senseless repetition of words or phrases) (Andersen, Dunlea and Kekelis 1984). Various theories of echolalia have been advanced (for example, Fraiberg 1977). In terms of the three-strand model of functional hearing set out above, echolalia can be interpreted as the transfer of music-structural techniques (the repetition of sounds or qualities of sound) to the verbal domain, whereby the sounding qualities of words are treated as abstract properties to be manipulated free of any semantic ties. In fact, as we shall see, music can be a powerful tool in promoting the development of language, and, ironically, the very repetition that underpins echolalia can be used in musical contexts to help children move beyond it.

Music

As well as being a source of pleasure in its own right, exposure to music – the art of organized sound – can assist in developing a number of aspects of listening skills, depending on the type of music involved (Ockelford 1998). So, from the earliest stages, consider introducing children to pieces in a variety of styles. There are a great number of possibilities: from fugues to folksongs, for example, from symphonies to spirituals, and ragtime to rap, involving acoustic and electronic instruments ranging from the piano to the panpipes, the drum kit to the didgeridoo, and the gamelan to the electric guitar. Live performances may well have a greater impact than recordings: being near a band, orchestra, choir or solo performer in full flow can be electrifying.

It has been suggested that congenitally blind children in particular may have an unusual propensity to develop an interest in music and, as a consequence, to develop exceptional musical abilities. For example, among a group of 50 children blind since birth or shortly afterwards who attended a special school in London in the 1980s, 20 (40 per cent) had 'perfect pitch', the very unusual ability to recognize or produce notes in isolation that normally occurs in around one in 10,000 of the population (Ockelford 1988). Moreover, around half these children had learning difficulties in addition to their visual impairment, and three were classified as 'musical savants' (people with exceptional musical talent in the context of learning difficulties) (Ockelford 2000b). The most prevalent eye conditions of those with perfect pitch were retinopathy of prematurity, Leber's amaurosis and septo-optic dysplasia. Hence, parents of children with these conditions, in particular, may wish to be alert to the possibility of the development of unusual sound-processing abilities in a musical context. Remember, though, that such abilities may, but need not, be part of a more generally evolving musicality.

David was born three-and-a-half months premature, and, in the course of the intensive efforts to keep him alive that followed, his retinas were irreparably damaged, leaving him only with the perception of light in one eye. During the first two years of life, it also became clear that David had global developmental delay, with severe learning difficulties and problems in processing language. However, he showed a consistently strong interest in music, listening intently and with unfailing concentration whenever a CD was played, for example. Then, when he was 30 months, his mother and father noticed something remarkable: David started to pick out tunes on his little keyboard they had bought him, and that he had been exploring entirely on his own since he was about one-and-a-half. Through a support group, David's parents made contact with a teacher who specialized in working with children with special abilities and needs, and she devised a programme for David that both promoted the development of his musical talents as well as using music to support his emerging cognitive, linguistic and social skills. To this day, music remains a central feature of David's life: now in his mid-twenties, playing the piano brings him immense personal satisfaction as well as providing a vehicle for socialising with a wide range of other people.

Blind and partially sighted children may take part in music-making of any type and at any level, and parents and teachers are referred to other publications for detailed accounts of the acquisition of vocal and instrumental technique with little or no sight, specialized notation in large print or braille, learning by ear and approaches to playing in groups (Ockelford 1996a). Here, we consider how music-listening skills can be used to promote other areas of development: movement, learning, language, and socialization (Ockelford 2000a).

From around the age of 6 months, babies will typically move spontaneously to music (Moog 1976). Later, the movements that children make in response to pieces may be freely expressive, or characteristics of the music they are listening to may determine, more or less specifically, the actions that accompany it. Hence music can provide an auditory frame of reference for movement, something that may be particularly significant for those who have no visual model to guide them, or to clarify what may be a confusing picture of events for others who have little sight. The strongest link between music and movement is to be found in rhythm, which sets the pace for action, although other connections are possible too. For example, loud sounds may be associated with large movements and quiet sounds with small ones. A rise in pitch is widely considered to correspond to movement in an upward direction, and vice versa. While this correspondence is generally conveyed through the more or less conscious efforts of teachers and others, there is some evidence that it also occurs as a natural part of the way thinking develops in blind and sighted children alike (Welch 1991).

Music can promote wider learning in a number of ways. For example, purposefully listening to pieces engages concentration and memory, and such engagement may transfer to other areas of experience, particularly those that also involve listening (Bunt 1994). Other concepts may be extracted from the experience of music too, such as the opposing notions of 'quiet' and 'loud', 'slowly' and 'quickly', and 'the same' and 'different'. Objects may be identified through their sound-making qualities and classified accordingly. For instance, children may be encouraged to contrast the ringing, bell-like sounds of metal with the more mellow resonance of wood, and to sort items on this basis. Conversely, supplementary auditory information may be incorporated more or less permanently into the environment. A room may be identified through a distinctive set of wind-chimes suspended in the doorway, for instance. Finally, note that all pieces of music and musical instruments are ultimately products of the society in which they originated, and offer a rich source of cultural information for children who are blind or partially sighted.

Music and words are closely linked products of the human psyche, enjoying a special relationship that from time immemorial has found expression in songs and chants. This affinity can be particularly useful in promoting the development of language in visually impaired children. From the earliest stages, for example, exposure to music may elicit vocalization (Moog 1976), and those working with youngsters who have special needs may exploit this tendency to promote the production and control of vocal sounds. Later, music can play a significant role in motivating children to use language, through the many songs that have been especially written or have evolved over the years for their edification and pleasure. Whether nursery rhymes or counting songs, playground chants or action songs, game songs or songs that tell a story, music adds another dimension to the verbal messages presented, enlivening everyday expressions and imbuing them with extra colour and interest. Music can also assist in structuring language. This may be particularly important for children who are blind or partially sighted and have learning difficulties, who may have to contend with a baffling array of different words and phrases for concepts that in any case they only imperfectly understand. Yet what children seeking order and regularity need most is simplicity and consistency. Here, music can help. By setting selected phrases to characteristic snatches of melody, reinforced where appropriate with other augmentative communication such as signing and objects of reference, the consistent delivery of key messages is assured (Ockelford 1996b). That is not to say that carefully structured musical fragments should be all that is communicated, but that they should form salient features in a rich and diverse landscape of multisensory interaction. By allocating important words and phrases short tunes of their own, one form of complex auditory input (speech) is supplemented with a simpler overlay (melody). The message is given a stronger identity, which is consequently more memorable, and which blind and partially sighted children with learning difficulties may find easier to recognize.

Music sessions offer a unique and secure framework through which many of the skills and disciplines of social interaction can be experienced and developed. This is particularly true for youngsters who are visually impaired, whose awareness of other people may be more than usually reliant on the sounds they make. Teachers, therapists and carers may provide structured opportunities for children to listen to the sounds that others are making, in a variety of contexts, and to respond appropriately to them. Music can be particularly effective in supporting the development of early social interaction. It is, as we have noted, highly repetitive (Ockelford 2004a): pieces are generally made up of sequences of identical or similar events, which divide time into manageable chunks, and constitute predictable patterns. Hence, it provides a secure framework for the risky business of reaching out into the far from predictable world of other people, setting parameters and establishing the boundaries within which socialization can occur, and building confidence through a medium which the great majority of children find enjoyable and motivating. Finally, it is worth remembering that musical activities give young people who are visually impaired the opportunity for experiencing a wide range of social situations. Music-making takes place indoors and outdoors, in concert halls and sitting rooms, with small groups of friends and among thousands of strangers. Each has its own sense of occasion and atmosphere. The key thing is for teachers and carers to find ways of offering visually impaired children fulfilling musical experiences: experiences which typically occur in the company of other people. Finally, remember that familiar music may offer individual emotional security too. A favourite tape at bedtime, for example, may comfort children who cannot see, in the same way that their fully sighted friends are reassured by glancing at well-known objects as they prepare to sleep: the gently repeating patterns of notes soothing the ear in the same way that the sleepy eye is calmed by tracing familiar images on the wallpaper.

Summary

For people with little or no sight, hearing assumes a greater importance than would otherwise be the case. However, visual impairment does not automatically lead to the development of superior hearing skills, and there are a number of strategies that parents and carers can use to support blind and partially sighted children in learning to use their hearing to best effect. Those offering such support should bear in mind that sound fulfils three distinct functions, in

Visual Needs

◆ everyday life

◆ speech, and

◆ music

which are processed in different ways. Children usually rely on vision as they learn to make sense of everyday sounds and speech, and sometimes, particularly if they have learning difficulties in addition to a visual impairment, the different strands of auditory development can become confused. For example, if children do not understand what words mean (or that they mean anything), they may treat them rather like the abstract sounds of music, and combine them using music-structural principles – particularly repetition – rather then linking them syntactically to form linguistically coherent utterances. There is much that can be done to assist children in this position, though, and music itself is one of the main tools available to parents and carers. It provides a predictable (and therefore safe) context for communication, ensures consistency in verbal exchanges, potentially offers alternative neurological pathways for the processing of language, and, above all, can be a great source of pleasure and motivation.

3

A Touching Sensation

Being able to explore the world through the integration of all our senses brings our vision of the world alive. Our sense of touch, like our vision, is sometimes under our conscious control and sometimes it is not. In Chapter 1 we made an artificial distinction between sight and vision and, in particular, the role of the dorsal and ventral streams within the brain in helping us to process visual information. It is also helpful to analyse touch in a similar way. We consciously reach out actively to touch objects but are also surrounded by things in the environment which touch us. We might therefore think of touch divided into conscious 'action' and received 'sensation'.

The sensation of touch is found all over our body and originates in the lower layer of skin called the dermis. The dermis is filled with numerous small nerve endings that transmit information via the spinal cord to the brain. Touch sensitivity varies in different parts of the body depending on the number of nerve endings present in any one area. The tip of the tongue, lips and fingertips are three of the most sensitive areas. There are about twenty or so different types of nerve endings but the most common are those that respond to pressure, pain, warmth and cold. There is a specific kind of receptor for each of what are described as the cutaneous senses. For example, light-touch receptors convey only the sensation that an object is in contact with the body, while those receptors which respond to pressure convey the force, or extent, of that contact.

One of the most common examples used when describing touch is the role of braille in the lives of people who are blind and the use of fingertips in feeling the raised shapes (dots) of the braille code. However, the more subtle aspects of touch, such as the movement of air against the body and changes in air temperature, all provide important information about our environment. For instance, a child who has little or no sight can be taught to utilize the airflow around a building as a useful navigational cue.

Susanna Millar (1994) suggests the major differences between vision and touch are often neglected. Because reaching and touching happen so early in our development they are deeply interlinked with vision. We are not conscious of the different activity involved, but as Millar points out the 'where' and 'what' so integrated in a visual response can be uncoupled when one relies on touch. Touch alone does not give us sufficient information to build up the 'what' but plenty of information to find out the 'where'.

We therefore need additional contextual information to build up our object and spatial understanding. This information primarily comes from vision, but when vision is absent or impaired the 'complementary' information we need must come from other forms of sensory input. As described earlier there are important distinctions to be made between 'action' and 'sensation'. As the term 'active touch' implies we use this form of touch to find out what is around us. In order to do this our touch becomes exploratory so we can build up our understanding of objects and their position in space. The information we receive is logged in a sort of 'sensory database' of experiences, thus building memories for future comparison, identification and reference. The outcome of this process, combined with information from other sources, promotes our understanding of what is happening around us. 'Haptic perception' is the term used to describe this process. There are numerous ways in which we use our hands to find out tactual information and these depend on the shapes we are trying to explore. The 'pincer grip' is a particularly important physical skill that enables us to pick up very small objects. It is also critical in allowing us to explore the detail of larger objects. Sometimes it is necessary to bring both hands together. Braille requires very fine motor control in our fingers while the use of a Perkins Brailler to produce braille requires strong and supple fingerwork. Much of the early work with children who will later become braillists focuses on what are described as 'pre-braille' skills aimed at developing effective discrimination by touch and increasing the strength and coordination of fingers and hands. But the process of active touch can sometimes be disrupted or disturbed as in the cases of Simon and Emma. Simon is using touch but seems to be gaining very little from the experience while Emma actively avoids touch.

Simon is 3 and totally blind. He was born prematurely and had a very low birth-weight and a condition known as retinopathy of prematurity (ROP). Simon has never had any useful sight but moves around his environment at a furious pace. He often bumps into objects but just carries on regardless. Simon's mother dreads taking him to the supermarket because he touches everything with quick, sometimes destructive, hand movements and seems to gather very little information from the objects around him. Simon is an only child and his behaviour is a constant worry for his mother. Simon's father feels that his son lacks discipline but Simon's mother argues that Simon may have learning difficulties and that he doesn't really understand why people sometimes get cross with him about his constant 'touching'. This difference in opinion between the parents sometimes causes friction at home.

Simon's use of touch does not seem to be helping him to find his way around or to explore with an obvious purpose. His hand movements are quick and his touch is fleeting. To an outside observer Simon would seem to have a major difficulty. Touch is considered such an important sense for people who are blind that questions arise about Simon's future. For instance, since Simon has been blind from birth and without purposeful touch will he ever be able to learn to read braille? How can his 'active touch' be developed so he can learn about the world around him? If we think again about the need for touch to be supported by complementary information, what might we be missing from Simon's environment? There may be some emotional factors to consider. Is Simon's behaviour really that different in the supermarket from that of other three year olds, or is his mother more conscious of it because of his blindness and the reaction of others? How might

Simon feel about going to a large place such as a super-market? He may be nervous or excited. We know his mother worries about taking Simon to the supermarket so perhaps this feeling is transmitted to him. More fundamentally, does Simon have the additional learning difficulty his mother suspects? There is some information we need to find out:

◆ What does Simon enjoy and when is he most relaxed?

◆ How does Simon behave at home?

◆ How is Simon introduced to new experiences?

◆ Does Simon have effective listening skills and how can we tell?

◆ What size and shape of objects does Simon choose to explore in the home environment – if any?

◆ How does Simon use his hands to search for objects or people?

◆ Has Simon developed a reliable pincer-grip?

◆ Does Simon try to communicate with those around him and how?

◆ How does Simon react when touched?

◆ Does Simon respond differently to different people?

◆ Does Simon remember and anticipate events?

In the case of Emma there are other factors. Emma simply refuses to touch anything that is presented to her.

Visual Needs

Emma is 3 years old and was born without any eyes (anophthalmos). Emma joined the nursery at her local school with support from a specialist teacher for pupils who are visually impaired. Emma loves to listen to music and has good verbal skills though much of what she says is repetitive. She does not interact with her peers. She is reluctant to move around the nursery area by herself and refuses to use her hands to explore toys or other objects. Lots of attempts have been made by nursery staff and by other children to encourage Emma to join in sand and water play but she resists and can become quite distressed. Emma is described as 'tactile defensive'. However, she will hold the hand of a familiar adult and will pull the adult in the direction of the outside door to the nursery where her grandmother waits to take her home. Because of Emma's seeming indifference to her environment this skill in orientation completely baffles the nursery staff.

For Emma as for Simon the world can be a frightening and confusing place where things happen quickly and experiences are often unpredictable. Although spending time in a nursery with other children is important, Emma needs to be introduced to this experience over a considerable period of time. It is not surprising that staff want Emma to be included in the sort of activities other children enjoy. It is also not surprising, given her blindness, that considerable emphasis is placed on Emma using her hands. But there may be perfectly logical reasons why Emma is resisting touch. Just as some young children will look away or close their eyes when faced with a new person or experience, perhaps Emma is trying to make a choice about what stimulation she can accommodate and in what sort of circumstance. There is, after all, a vast difference in being touched and reaching out to touch. The partnership between home and nursery or playgroup is key to finding ways of understanding how Emma responds and how best to intervene. From discussion with parents or carers it is possible to find out:

◆ In what circumstances Emma will tolerate touch

◆ If there are any particular textures or surfaces in the home environment that Emma will explore independently and if so how

◆ If Emma has any siblings and how she responds and interacts with them

◆ If there have been any particular incidents or changes at home or in the nursery that might have upset Emma

◆ If there are any playthings which Emma is happy to touch without prompting

◆ If Emma has any physical problems, which might make being touched, or touching objects difficult or uncomfortable

◆ If Emma's apparent verbal skill is making people assume she understands more than is actually the case

◆ If Emma's skill in moving towards the outside door can be built on and extended

Summary

In this section we have described some of the ways in which the process of touch operates and have divided touch into two broad though interrelated aspects of 'action' and 'sensation'. Through the case studies of Simon and Emma we have examined some difficulties faced by children who have been blind from birth and raised a number of questions we might need answered in order to understand the needs of these children. In particular, we have highlighted the following:

◆ Touch is complex and the action of touching may not come easily to some children who are visually impaired

◆ Resisting touch may be a perfectly logical way for a child who is visually impaired to respond

◆ Touch is not always a conscious exploration of the environment

◆ Children who are visually impaired may be using the subtle movement of air or the changes in temperature to orientate themselves in a room

◆ Motivation is a key factor in the use of information from touch

◆ Learning difficulties may arise from lack of environmental awareness, or conversely such difficulties may prevent or impair children's ability to access and process the information around them

◆ Getting to know a child over time and observing changes in behaviour will help those involved to understand the way the child is using information from touch

◆ Emotional factors play an ongoing part in the development of children who are visually impaired

◆ Communication between home and nursery/school is vital

4

A Sensory Illusion: the Case of Taste and Smell

The information received from our senses is complex and can be illusory. The case of the relationship between taste and smell is a good example both of complexity and illusion. Although the sensations of taste and smell seem specific and distinct there is now plenty of agreement between researchers that different areas of our brain play an essential part in helping us to create the whole sensory experience. For instance, vision plays a major part in how we perceive taste just as 80–90 per cent of taste (especially the flavour of food) is actually triggered by our sense of smell. The sense of smell is a primal sense in humans and animals and is fundamental to the way we gather information from our environment and how our environment communicates with us. There is evidence that babies start learning smells in the womb. Smells are highly evocative. For example, the familiar smell of a favourite food triggers a memory of past meals and thus the anticipation of pleasure, while the smell of smoke can trigger a fear of fire and alert us to possible danger.

By comparison to our sense of smell, our ability to taste is limited. The tongue is lined with only five different types of taste buds and these respond to sour, salty, bitter, sweet and meaty tastes, whereas we can tell the difference between 4,000–10,000 different smells. Our sense of touch is also a factor in taste as the tongue plays an important part in sensing the texture and temperature of food. The tip of the tongue is one of the most touch-sensitive parts of the body (see Chapter 3). In fact, all our senses combine to make eating a meal or enjoying the scent of a flower part of an ongoing multisensory experience.

Ian is 4 and in the summer he loves to go for a walk with his father in the local park. Although Ian has very limited vision he has memorized his favourite route because he loves ice cream, and the smell of lavender is an important reminder of his favourite treat. In the park there are lavender bushes planted along the side of the path he uses to reach the end of the flower-beds. At the end of the flower-beds Ian knows he and his father always turn right and the next stop is the ice cream van where his father usually buys him an ice cream.

All very young children during the early stages of development will use their mouths and particularly their tongues to explore objects. As manual dexterity, vision and reaching become more precise and language develops, so the oral dominance in exploration fades. But for some children with a severe visual impairment, particularly when this visual impairment is combined with other needs, this form of exploratory behaviour may persist. In many ways the mouth, particularly the tongue, is gathering similar information to that normally provided through other tactual and visual routes.

Nazreen is almost 6 and has a cortical visual impairment combined with a severe physical disability. Nazreen explores her environment by bottom shuffling and as she moves she reaches out and brings objects to her mouth. Some objects she discards very quickly but others seem to interest her and she is careful to run her mouth and tongue over their surface. Nazreen is still at a very early stage in communication but makes clear choices using oral exploration.

An extended period of oral exploration may also be accompanied by a rejection of certain textures in food. For example, some children will only tolerate dry foods, while others will reject even the tiniest lump in their food. This can make mealtimes difficult but it is important to set these preferences within the context of a sensitivity of touch rather than 'feeding fussiness'. Speech and language therapists with experience of the needs of children who have a severe visual impairment can offer practical advice to support parents and professionals on the development of individual feeding plans designed to make mealtimes part of a communication programme. Input from the peripatetic (itinerant) teacher of pupils who are visually impaired will address other issues such as lighting, contrast and possible approaches to using smell and texture as part of a structured programme of sensory stimulation.

Instead of preventing oral exploration we need to find additional ways of helping children to find complementary strategies for understanding and interacting with their environment. This is vital in the development of effective forms of communication (speech, gesture or sign) and as an aid to concept formation. We also need to recognize that the loss or impairment of the major distance sense of vision has to be replaced or supplemented by additional emphasis on the other senses. However, sensory input has to be integrated to be fully effective in providing a multisensory experience. Sensory integration may happen spontaneously for some children with a visual impairment but for others the process of sensory stimulation and integration will need to be fostered by careful observation, planning, empathy and imagination.

Summary

In this chapter we have outlined the links between smell, taste and vision as part of an integrated multisensory experience. We have drawn attention to the need for:

◆ Recognition of the importance of the olfactory process (smell/taste) in helping to evoke memories, promote understanding, concept formation and communication

◆ Empathy, careful observation, planning and imagination to foster sensory integration

◆ Awareness that prolonged oral exploration by children who are visually impaired (particularly those with multiple needs) is a natural response by the child to sensory deprivation

A Sensory Illusion: the Case of Taste and Smell

◆ Investigation of the link between texture sensitivity and the rejection of some types of food

◆ Advice and assessment from a speech and language therapist

Part Two

Agency: Interacting with the World

5

Making Contact

In the first moments after birth an intricate interaction begins between mother and baby. The baby is born with a sophisticated sensory system that enables her to establish a visual rapport with her carer and the ability to use sound and touch to elicit attention. During the early months this interaction between carer and child becomes a subtle interplay with both using all means available to them to make contact. By the time a baby is two weeks old her carer will already be able to hear a difference between her general comfort crying and more specific hunger or discomfort sounds. The baby in turn will respond more readily to a female voice than to other types of sound (see Chapter 2).

Initially the world of the newborn baby is close. We know that vision is an important part of that world. Much of the early interaction between baby and carer is prompted by the child's ability to look at her carers and copy their facial movements (see Chapter 1). Touch is also vitally important during the early months and the baby will establish and receive physical contact with her carer. The close proximity of all these major interactions provides the baby with a natural order and structure to her environment. The baby can later build on this security and consistency in order to anticipate what is about to happen and to establish the foundations of communication. For a baby who has little or no sight, the world of sound gains prominence (see Chapter 2). Adults naturally tend to use a different, higher tone of voice when speaking to babies and young children and the tone of voice used with babies who are visually impaired is even more significant. For instance, the smile on the face of a carer has to be carried through her voice.

In those first days after we came home from the hospital I began to understand her needs. It was difficult at first because she couldn't see me and I couldn't tell if she knew I was there. Very soon I learnt that she could find what she needed by instinct. Now she turns towards my breast in anticipation when wanting to be fed, responds to my touch when I cuddle her and seems soothed by the sound of my voice. I feel we are gradually getting to know each other.

Communication is a two-way process. To hold a conversation requires something much like mind reading. Both parties involved in a conversation have to be paying attention. If you say to me, 'Look at that!' I have to know which 'that' you are referring to. I have to know where and what it is, I have to understand that you know these things too and I have to understand that when you say, 'Look at this!' that 'that' is history and 'this' is what we are talking about now. This shows how complex even a simple conversation can actually be. When communication shifts from 'that' to 'this' to something else again, there is a danger that young children with visual impairments will become confused.

One of the teachers in the nursery was telling the story of 'The Enormous Turnip'. Suzy listened carefully. She had very little sight so couldn't see the gestures made by the teacher. When asked about the story it became clear that she had no idea what a turnip was and thought it was a large animal.

Talking about the world (building on essential communication)

Most things we use in everyday life have a small set of functions and purposes, and young children have to learn what these are. It seems to be a general rule of early learning that you have to know how to break something utterly before you really gain a sense of how to use it properly. Books, for example, as well as being looked at and read, can also be nibbled, crayoned in, torn to tatters or fed to the nearest available video recorder. So by the time they enter school, most children have had opportunities to find out about the properties of the things around them – and, most importantly, to talk about them. They know, for example, that when the ball rolls behind the sofa it does not vanish into thin air, and they know that glass is fragile, so they'd better be careful. Children with visual difficulties are less likely to have had such a rich variety of experiences and will possibly have a smaller repertoire of communication skills with which to engage with others about the things they have discovered. They are therefore likely to need particular help on the road to formal communication.

Formal communication is generally understood as the use of speech or sign language, reading or writing. But formal communication also includes other approaches such as finger spelling and the use of symbols (visual or tactile) and, increasingly, technology. Generally a formal communication-user will communicate in sentences and part sentences, rather than single words, though even skilled formal communicators are known to use grunts, shrugs and dramatic sighs, especially during adolescence!

Formal communicators can talk about ideas and events beyond their immediate environment and experience. Many young children who are blind from birth have very advanced speech and are skilled in formal communication. But for some this verbal skill can lack real understanding of the concepts involved, and in such cases speech may be largely echolalic (see Chapter 2). Much as the sighted children learn by copying facial expressions they also learn by copying adult speech and will 'parrot' back an expression they have heard. As the child's own powers of expression develop then echolalia fades.

> I asked Ben which drink he would like. 'Would you like the apple or orange?' Ben replied 'apple or orange'. I then poured one small cup of apple and one of orange and let Ben smell each. Without hesitation he took the orange drink and smiled.

When a child lacks experience as a result of a sensory deprivation such as visual impairment then concept formation can be delayed. Even when children who have never had any sight have a good level of concept formation they can still ask what might seem rather bizarre questions.

Leo was talking to his mother and she was explaining that his sister was in the next room. Leo wanted to know what his sister was doing. His mother said that she didn't know, as she couldn't see her. Leo asked why and his mother explained that the walls were solid and that even with sight you couldn't see through solid walls. She then had to explain about windows and that although you could feel the glass you could still see through the window. To show Leo the difference she walked Leo round the house so he could feel and hear the difference between the windows and the walls.

We were driving through the park and it was raining. I told Isabella that there were deer in the park but I couldn't see them at the moment because they were under the trees. Isabella seemed confused and asked why deer got under trees. I realized that her lack of visual experience meant she wasn't able to imagine what I meant and so needed more explanation. I stopped the car as soon as I could and together with Isabella walked to a large tree. We stood under the tree and Isabella was able to feel the difference between being out in the open in the rain and then under the tree. She could also hear the sound of the rain as it fell on the leaves above her. She already knew about deer from a visit to a local zoo so she then understood what I had been trying to explain.

It is easy to assume that children who are visually impaired share our understanding of what we are trying to tell them, but the experiences of Suzy, Leo and Isabella indicate that this might not be the case. To help we need to:

Visual Needs

◆ Back up any spoken information using examples from the child's experience

◆ Use props which children can feel to help them understand (ideally the 'real thing')

◆ Check that the child understands prepositions such as 'under', 'above', etc.

◆ Remember that many children with little or no sight have no idea about the scale of objects so it is important to find ways to show them, for example, how small an insect might be when compared to a bird or cat

◆ Use additional sensory information – for example, the sound of rain, the smell of a drink, the texture of glass as opposed to brick

◆ Listen carefully to children when they ask questions and try to respond as soon as possible rather than waiting

◆ If a child asks the same question repeatedly (sometimes without listening to your answer!), think why he or she might be doing it; for instance, it may be to gain or retain your attention

◆ Listen to the way children talk to each other to understand better the way they think and relate to their peers

◆ Help children learn to find things out for themselves

Trust and security: using clearly structured, consistent routines

Trust and security are preconditions for successful communication: there are only a very few things you really need in order to feel safe and secure and to be able to trust the people with you. Familiar settings and activities with well-established, predictable routines that make the child comfortable are the essential underpinnings of successful, positive communication. For instance, the routines offered by mealtimes provide invaluable opportunities for communication. By offering a choice of food or drink children can be encouraged to communicate their preferences as in the case of Ben. Routines can also help the child to feel part of a group.

> For our Circle Time, we (the staff) always sit by the 'Good morning' board, as this has the children's names in tactile form, objects and photographs, which we use throughout this activity. The children always use the same props and we sit next to the same child every time we do this, to keep the continuity.

Although we have stressed the importance of routines in the development of trust and security it is also necessary to help the child to understand that routines may be changed or interrupted. We need to use the routine to help the child to cope with the unexpected (for example, if a key worker is away). Adapting to change can be difficult for many children. However, some children with visual impairments and complex needs can become so dependent on a particular routine that they resist even the slightest change.

Visual Needs

Communication skills may then be restricted by the lack of new experience and interaction. A routine should therefore be about helping the child to gain confidence in her communication skills and helping her to organize her environment so that she can feel in control. The child needs to be involved in the development of a routine so adults should avoid taking all the decisions and remember that:

◆ Each step is a key decision point; without it the routine will not progress

◆ The child takes the lead, making decisions at a level appropriate to her

◆ The adult's role is to support the child in making these decisions

Summary

In this chapter we have drawn attention to the various stages in the development of communication and the possible impact of a visual impairment.

In particular, we have concentrated on the need for:

◆ Understanding and meeting the child's visual needs

◆ Sensory access – through vision, hearing, touch and movement

◆ Communication access – building on existing communication skills

◆ The use of clearly structured and consistent routines aimed at fostering the confidence of the child

◆ Being consistent in the type of language used to describe objects and people

But most importantly we have emphasized that communication is a two-way process with both partners playing an active role. We have also stressed the importance of listening rather than directing the child, and responding so the child feels she has something worthwhile to communicate and that she is understood.

6

Play and Independence

Play is the joyful, inspired, improvised testing of as many possibilities as you can think of. Play is not 'What am I meant to do with this thing?' Play is 'What *can* I do with this thing?' Play is about exploration, communication and imagination. Play is also about seeing the world through the eyes of others and sharing a sense of exploration and delight. Play is how children become competent in the world; how they develop ways of dealing with situations and difficulties they have not encountered before, or prepared for in advance. Being competent, being able to deal with the world we encounter helps us to use all of our abilities and to become independent human beings.

Vision is usually integral to this process. It provides a bridge between our other senses. More significantly, it is the most obvious factor in the development of mutual interest between caregivers and children. Vision is especially important in allowing children easy access to their environment, and when combined with touch and hearing, vision normally plays an important part in the development of early pleasurable interactions with a caregiver.

As we support children in the development of play and independence, we will always be most effective if we understand how they learn. Does the child best learn through direct, real activities? Is she able to use her imagination to 'make believe', bringing into her play ideas from stories? Is she able to share in a group activity, or is she too easily distracted and confused by this? What is it that the child is learning; is it control of her surrounding world, or that others can share this exploration with her, or is she combining these two aspects of learning to learn through organized topics and activities? Does she adapt easily to a number of different adults and settings, or require a less complex routine? How does she use her vision and other senses? Is vision her most effective sense? If so, what helps or hinders her ability to use her vision? If vision is not her main sensory route for learning, which is? Does this change, depending on the activity and on how familiar it and the accompanying people are?

Settings and opportunities for play and learning

By thinking about different aspects of play we can see what it is that interests children who are visually impaired. We can then use this as the foundation for choosing activities that they will enjoy, and find relevant and interesting. Children may be discovering that they can become active explorers within their environment by themselves. They may be developing their play and independence in the company of another child, or with an adult. They may be using what they have learnt about their world to take a meaningful part in a group. Successful play and independence is promoted through developing a sense of trust and security, building relationships, offering and sharing play experiences, as well as learning through movement and music.

For instance, we know that children who have been blind from birth are less interested in toys that are models of the real world. A tactile experience of a toy horse often bears little resemblance to the 'real thing'. Meaningful first-hand experience for visually impaired children therefore has to involve real things as much as possible. Objects which offer more significant 'hands-on' reward are those which have a clear function. Real wooden spoons (preferably ones that have actually been used to mix cakes or whatever) are therefore more meaningful than toy spoons which offer a symbolic significance to a sighted child but little interest to a child who has never been able to see. Textures are also important and many young children who are visually impaired will prefer smooth and hard textures to the soft, fluffy toy animals that many sighted children love, since they do not have a definite feel or shape.

It is important to remember that very few children have no sight at all and so toys that offer a visual reward may also be important for direct experience. Children in the early stages of visual development are likely to be especially interested in bold patterns, bright light and movement. However, for some children a severe visual loss can mean opportunities for play and independence can be restricted by:

◆ Poor mobility

◆ Self stimulatory behaviours

◆ Limited exploratory behaviour

Visual Needs

◆ Poor play rewards from available toys or activities

◆ Limited opportunities to be creative

◆ Fewer shared experiences

Taking time to observe children

In a busy nursery, classroom or even in the home, adults can feel uncomfortable when not actively intervening in a child's play because just 'looking' is sometimes equated with idleness. We can find ourselves blundering ahead with no notion of what we are going to do, because getting on and doing something – anything – *feels* like we are achieving something, even when we are not. Children with visual difficulties may need settings for play and learning that allows them to experience a range of carefully orchestrated opportunities. Observation of the child can help us to understand what type of intervention (if any) we should be offering the child and when to stand back and allow the child to find out by herself.

Places where children can become active explorers, by themselves and with others

Sometimes a severe visual impairment may mean a child becomes 'stuck' in a passive relationship with the world around her – only responding, never making things happen themselves. Typically, children are *not* passive; they are all endless curiosity and wonder in the presence of new things to discover or when returning to old favourites. The confidence, inquisitiveness and creativity bubbling through them has as its bedrock a sense of trust and security and the ability to predict accurately what is likely to happen next.

In the mother and toddler group, Charlie was largely happy to explore his surroundings with his mother nearby.

Charlie was confident because he felt secure in the knowledge that his mother was near him. He had begun to use his widening curiosity to learn about his environment and his mother used every opportunity to help him. For instance, Charlie was encouraged to explore his home and learn about traffic during walks to his gran's house.

What we can do to help

◆ Provide enough time for children to take part in meaningful exploration and play

◆ Give enough time for children to register the beginning and end of an activity, before moving on to the next thing

◆ Provide one-to-one settings, which are physically well-defined, not too big for children to discover the overall size, and that promote a feeling of trust and safety

◆ Provide settings free from distractions such as interruption and intrusion by other people (adults and children alike), and that allow children to concentrate on their immediate sensory environment without the added confusion of the sound, movement and the general bustle of other learners

◆ Ensure children have enough opportunity to become aware of your presence. Do not dash to and fro, but stay with them from the beginning through most, if not all, of the session

◆ Establish and use clear, consistent routines

◆ Ensure daily opportunities for exploratory play

Play and learning with other children

It is important to remember always that children with visual needs are children first and foremost. An essential feature of their play and learning is that it reflects the experiences of their typically developing siblings and friends. But just leaving children who are visually impaired with other children is not the same as helping them to be involved actively in collaborative play.

Although Michael cannot see much of what is happening in the pretend game of baby minding, he has learnt that it is important to follow the rules of make-believe. Because he has quite sophisticated communication skills he now knows that he is expected to feed the 'baby'. At first he was puzzled because the doll didn't feel like a baby and there was no food on the pretend spoon but now he joins in with the others and uses his love of stories and sounds to enhance the game.

For some children collaborative play remains difficult. Children with visual and multiple needs often continue to have very adult-orientated interactions. This may be because of their early levels of cognitive and physical functioning but does this mean that play with other children is impossible? Are there additional barriers that prevent such play? The large and isolating pieces of equipment some children use is one factor, as can be the very individualized learning and therapy programmes they follow. The demands of the curriculum and the constraints of staffing and time also play their part, but so also does our adult perception of what constitutes interaction between peers. If an adult is there as an over-directive presence, children may not be able to engage with each other in childlike ways.

> Peter is being introduced to pre-braille work which involves matching textures. He is completely separate from the rest of the class. One little girl is obviously keen to be his partner, but no opportunity is given so she gives up and sits with another child. Peter cannot see her and is not aware of her interest and so continues with his task alone.

Similarly, if a child's level of play and exploration is significantly different from that of the other children in his group, he will have few chances to truly share with them. Sometimes the behaviour of a child who has a severe visual loss can seem very disturbing to adults and can prevent the child's interaction with other children.

> Andrew is very absorbed in what he is doing and appears to be quite oblivious to the other children in the nursery. Andrew spends much of his time rocking backwards and forwards.

Behaviours such as the rocking motion displayed by Andrew are described as 'stereotypic'. These behaviours take the form of repetitive actions such as rocking, hand flapping and eye poking. Stereotypic behaviour tends to increase when:

◆ A child is understimulated

◆ A child is overstimulated

◆ A child is tired

◆ A child is ill

◆ A child is anxious

Stereotypic behaviour prevents the child from engaging in what is happening around her. But there are also behaviours that are superficially similar to stereotypic behaviour but are in fact a sign that the child is concentrating. It is important not to confuse the two forms of behaviour.

Nadim is listening to the story and is really concentrating. As he listens he presses his fist into his eye socket. Immediately staff see this they take his hand away from his eye. Consequently Nadim loses concentration and becomes upset.

Nadim does not know his habit of eye pressing is disturbing to those around him. Observation of the child will help those around him to understand if a particular behaviour is helping or preventing the child from engaging with what is happening. Great sensitivity is required to prevent the child becoming overly self-conscious.

Play and independence with an accompanying adult

As communication partners with children who have little or no sight, we often have to use special strategies to ensure that information can be passed from child to adult and adult to child. We have to make what we do far more obvious and have to take more time to ensure messages are sent and received. Most importantly, we have to be prepared to engage with what interests the child more often than what interests us. One of the main things to make more explicit is the finishing of an event. This serves two purposes: it tells the child the activity has finished and it says that the topic of conversation or game is about to change. These social cues help the child to learn how to respond and encourage the child's understanding of socially acceptable behaviour.

What we can do to help

◆ Give lots of time

◆ Offer experiences but do not take over and try to lead things

◆ Ensure children can explore objects as directly as possible using the senses from which they gain the most meaning

◆ Organize activities through routines

◆ Always provide young children with more than one thing (lots of things in fact) to do – you cannot assume that you will know what they will be interested in from one occasion to another

The physical environment

The physical environment can support a child's play and independence in a number of ways, but a key function is helping to create a sense of security. The environment can also provide clues to an activity that is about to happen. It can be a place to explore and discover, and a space in which objects and people are contained, helping to define their physical relationship one to another. The clues provided by an environment also help a child to follow routes, whether from one part of a classroom to another, between rooms, or on longer journeys around a school or home and later to regular and familiar destinations in the local community.

One of the most popular play environments is often just a large cardboard box.

Debbie found the large cardboard box in the corner of the nursery. She was delighted with her find and crawled inside. She loved the fact that she could easily reach the sides and top of the box. Other children in the nursery also enjoyed the security of the box and wanted to join her. Debbie had become quite territorial and needed to be encouraged to share her space.

A consistent layout is important for many children regardless of the size of the space involved.

This activity occurs in the structured environment of the Nursery. There are many toys positioned around the Nursery, on the floor and on shelves and in cupboards throughout the classroom – all these at heights accessible to the children.

The area used for music is a large, well-lit space with good acoustics and plenty of natural lighting from windows spanning the breadth of the sidewalls.

Summary

In this chapter we have described the importance of play for laying the foundations of independence and also as a means of socialization. As in other chapters we have drawn attention to the need for predictability and routine in order to foster the child's sense of security. We have also emphasized the importance of exploratory play, choice making and a sense of 'being in control'. To reinforce and stimulate the interest of the child we have suggested it is important to provide:

◆ Good lighting

◆ Good acoustic environments

◆ Any necessary visual enhancement (low-vision aids such as magnification)

◆ Hands-on experience of real objects

◆ The opportunity to gather any additional information by using other senses (such as hearing, smell and taste)

◆ A key worker who can maintain consistent interaction with the child and who understands and is sensitive to a child's preferred mode of communication

Visual Needs

◆ A sensitive response to behaviours which may seem 'different' such as eye pressing, but which are important to the child nevertheless

We have emphasized the role of the adult as facilitator, by judging when to stand back and when to intervene.

References

Chapter 1 The Mysterious Case of Vision

Atkinson, J. (2000) *The Developing Visual Brain*, Oxford, Oxford University Press.

Groenveld, M. (1993) 'Effects of visual behaviour on development' in A. Fielder, A. Best and C. O. Bax (eds) *The Management of Visual Impairment in Childhood*, London, MacKeith Press.

Jan, J. E. and Freeman, R. D. (1998) 'Who is a visually impaired child?' *Developmental Medicine & Child Neurology*, 40, 65–7.

Chapter 2 Sound Track

Andersen, E., Dunlea, A. and Kekelis, L. (1984) 'Blind children's language: resolving some differences', *Journal of Child Language*, 11, 645–64.

Best, A. (1992) *Teaching Children with Visual Impairments*, Milton Keynes, Open University Press.

Bunt, L. (1994) *Music Therapy: An Art beyond Words*, London, Routledge

Cross, I. (2003) 'Music, cognition, culture and evolution', in I. Peretz and R. Zatorre (eds) *The Cognitive Neuroscience of Music*, Oxford, Oxford University Press, pp. 42–56.

References

Fassbender, C. (1996) 'Infants' auditory sensitivity towards acoustic parameters of speech and music', in J. Sloboda and I. Deliège (eds) *Musical Beginnings: Origins and Nature of Musical Competence*, Oxford, Oxford University Press, pp. 56–87.

Fauconnier, G. (1994) *Mental Spaces: Aspects of Meaning Construction in Natural Language*, Cambridge, Cambridge University Press

Fraiberg, S. (1977) *Insights from the Blind*, London, Souvenir Press.

Gaver, W. (1993) 'What in the world do we hear? An ecological approach to auditory event perception', *Ecological Psychology*, 5, 1–29.

Goldstein, E. (1999) *Sensation and Perception* (5th edn), Pacific Grove, CA, Brooks/Cole.

Harrison, F. and Crow, M. (1993) *Living and Learning with Blind Children: A Guide for Parents and Teachers of Visually Impaired Children*, Toronto, University of Toronto Press.

Juslin, P. and Sloboda, J. (2001) *Music and Emotion: Theory and Research*, Oxford, Oxford University Press.

Lecanuet, J.-P. (1996) 'Pre-natal auditory experience', in J. Sloboda and I. Deliège (eds) *Musical Beginnings: Origins and Nature of Musical Competence*, Oxford, Oxford University Press, pp. 3–34.

Lowenfeld, B. (1974) *The Visually Handicapped Child in School*, London, Constable.

Malloch, S. (1999/2000) 'Mothers and infants and communicative musicality', *Musicae Scientiae*, Special Issue, 29–54.

Minter, M., Hobson, P. and Pring, L. (1991) 'Recognition of vocally expressed emotion by congenitally blind children', *Journal of Visual Impairment and Blindness*, 85, 411–15.

Moog, H. (1976) *The Musical Experience of the Pre-School Child*, London, Schott.

Nielsen, L. (1992) *Educational Approaches for Visually Impaired Children*, Copenhagen, Sikon.

Ockelford, A. (1988) 'Some observations concerning the music education of blind children and those with additional handicaps', unpublished paper given at the 32nd conference of the Society for Research in Psychology of Music and Music Education, University of Reading.

——(1996a) *Music Matters: Factors in the Music Education of Children and Young People who are Visually Impaired*, London, Royal National Institute for the Blind.

——(1996b) *All Join in! A Framework for Making Music with Children and Young People who are Visually Impaired and have Learning Disabilities*, London, Royal National Institute for the Blind.

——(1998) *Music Moves: Music in the Education of Children and Young People who are Visually Impaired and have Learning Disabilities*, London, Royal National Institute for the Blind.

——(2000a) 'Music in the education of children with severe or profound learning difficulties: issues in current UK provision, a new conceptual framework, and proposals for research', *Psychology of Music*, 28, 197–217.

——(2000b) 'Savant-Syndrom oder-Syndrome? Fallstudien von jungen Menschen, die blind sind

References

und schwerwiegende Lernschwierigkeiten haben', invited paper at Musikalische Begabung und Expertise, Freiburg, Deutsche Gesellschaft für Musikpsychologie.

—— (2004a) *Repetition in Music: Theoretical and Metatheoretical Perspectives,* Royal Musical Association Monographs, No. 13, London, Ashgate.

—— (2004b) 'Musical structure, content and aesthetic response: Beethoven's Op. 110', *Journal of the Royal Musical Association*, (in press)

Scherer, K., Banse, R. and Wallbott, H. (2001) 'Emotion inferences from vocal expression correlate across languages and cultures', *Journal of Cross-Cultural Psychology*, 32, 76–92.

Sonksen, P. and Stiff, B. (1999) *Show me What my Friends can See: A Developmental Guide for Parents of Babies with Severely Impaired Sight and their Professional Advisors*, London, Institute of Child Health.

Thurman, L. and Welch, G. (2000) *Bodymind and Voice: Foundations of Voice Education,* Iowa City, IA, National Center for Voice and Speech.

Warren, D. (1984) *Blindness and Early Childhood Development* (2nd edn, revised), New York, American Foundation for the Blind.

Webster, A. and Roe, J. (1998) *Children with Visual Impairments: Social Interaction, Language and Learning*, London, Routledge.

Welch, G. (1991) 'Visual metaphors for sound: a study of mental imagery, language and pitch perception in the congenitally blind', *Canadian Journal of Research in Music Education*, 33, Special ISME Research Edition.

Wills, D. (1978) 'Early speech development in blind children', *The Psychoanalytic Study of the Child*, 32, 85–117.

Zimmermann, S. (1997) 'The mainstream curriculum: principles of access – music', in H. Mason and S. McCall (eds) *Visual Impairment: Access to Education for Children and Young People*, London, David Fulton, pp. 271–8.

Chapter 3 A Touching Sensation

Millar, S. (1994) *Understanding and Representing Space*, Oxford, Oxford University Press.

Bibliography

Allan, J. (1999) *Actively Seeking Inclusion*, London, Falmer Press.

Best A. B. (1992) *Teaching Children with Visual Impairments*, Milton Keynes, Open University Press.

Bowman, R. J. C., Bowman, R. F. and Dulton, G. (2001) *Disorders of Vision in Children*, London, RNIB.

Cunningham, C. and Davis, H. (1985) *Working with Parents: Frameworks for Collaboration*, Milton Keynes, Open University Press.

Dale, N. (1996) *Working with Families of Children with Special Needs. Partnership and Practice*, London, Routledge

Dawkins, J. (1992) *Models of Mainstream for Visually Impaired Children*, London, HMSO:

Edman, P. (1992) *Tactile Graphics*, New York, American Foundation for the Blind.

Fraiberg, S. (1977) *Insights from the Blind*, London, Souvenir Press (Human Horizons Series).

French, S. and Swain, J. (1997) *From a Different Viewpoint*, London, RNIB.

Hinton, R. (1996) *Tactile Graphics in Education*, Edinburgh, Moray House.

Hornby, G. (1995) *Working with Parents of Children with Special Needs*, London, Cassell

Bibliography

Leat, S. J., Shute, R. H. and Westall, C. A. (1999) *Assessing Children's Vision – A Handbook*, Oxford, Butterworth-Heinemann

Lewis, V. and Collis, G. M. (eds) (1997) *Blindness and Psychological Development in Young Children*, Leicester, BPS.

Mason, H. L. and McCall, S. (eds) (1997) *Visual Impairment: Access to Education for Children and Young People*, London, Fulton.

Miller, O. (1996) *Supporting the Visually Impaired Child in Mainstream School*, London, Franklin-Watts.

Murray, P. and Fielder, A. (1997) *Pocket Book of Ophthalmology*, Oxford, Butterworth-Heinemann

Ockelford, A. (1996) *Objects of Reference*, London, RNIB.

Perez Pereira, M. and Conti-Ramsden, G. (1999) *Language Development and Social Interaction in Blind Children*, Hove, Psychology Press.

RNIB (2001) *Access Technology*, London, RNIB.

Tobin, M. (1994) *Assessing Visually Handicapped People*, London, David Fulton.

Warren, D. H. (1994) *Blindness and Children*, Cambridge, Cambridge University Press.

Webster, A. and Roe J. (1998) *Children with Visual Impairments: Social Interaction, Language and Learning*, London, Routledge.